PERSONAL SAFETY FOR HEALTH CARE WORKERS

QUEEN'S UN
N.I. HEALTH

This book is the second in a series commissioned by The Suzy Lamplugh Trust.

Related titles:

Personal Safety for Social Workers
Personal Safety for Teachers

Published by
Arena
Ashgate Publishing Limited
Gower House
Croft Road
Aldershot
Hants GU11 3HR
England

Ashgate Publishing Company
Old Post Road
Brookfield
Vermont 05036
USA

British Library Cataloguing in Publication Data

Personal Safety for Health Care Workers
  I. Bibby, Pauline
  .362.88
ISBN 1 85742 196 5

Library of Congress Catalog Card Number: 95–76035

Typeset in 10pt Palatino by Bournemouth Colour Graphics Ltd. Printed in Great Britain by Hartnolls Ltd, Bodmin.

Personal Safety
for
Health Care Workers

Compiled and Edited by Pauline Bibby

Foreword by Diana Lamplugh OBE

arena

Contents

Foreword

by Diana Lamplugh OBE

Suzy left me a legacy. Nothing can take away the inevitable pain of her absence, that unfilled space in our lives which cuts to the quick. Nothing will change the fact that my daughter disappeared one sunny summer's midday while doing her normal work as a negotiator for an estate agency. Now, nearly nine years later, she has been presumed murdered, declared dead and we know we will never see her again. Now we have so many wonderful memories and we also have Suzy's legacy. This has touched many lives, has stayed the course of time and grown beyond any expectations.

It might appear remarkable, if it were not for the fact that her disappearance opened a festering wound which was already there. The problem of aggression and violence in the workplace was a present and growing concern, although at that time mainly unacknowledged or ignored. Gradually the tide of opinion has changed, the law has been redefined, EC directives have tightened up legislation, insurance companies are beginning to bite and the lawyers are responding to the scent of a possible new seam of profitable cases.

Now it is also commonly recognized that the professions are not immune. This has perhaps taken an even bigger leap of understanding. My father was in the law, my husband too was a lawyer who joined the staff of the Law Society. Even after our daughter disappeared I would never have considered that such a respectable profession could have a problem with personal safety.

These past eight years have forced me to think quite differently. With hindsight I realize how shaken my father was when faced with a shotgun when visiting a client in his country home. I now remember the time my father refused to prosecute the man who had deliberately scratched both sides of his car, 'The poor lad felt I let him down in his drink-driving case', he said. I thought of his receptionist tearing her hair out after the umpteenth call from an irate woman complaining about her neighbour and noise nuisance, and the articled clerk who was trapped into a blackmail situation over a property deal. All these incidents fall within the Health and Safety Executive and EC definitions of violence at work, which include verbal and mental abuse, discrimination, harassment, bullying and even ostracism as well as threats, assault and attack.

The night before we launched our manual *Training for Personal Safety in the Workplace*, I had been with a group of midwives in Cambridgeshire. Although the venue for my talk was in a hospital, most of those present worked in the community. As usual during my presentation we all swapped stories, and the ones I heard impressed me so much that when a journalist from *The Times* pressed me at the launch to say what kind of work or profession carried with it an element of risk, I did not hesitate to say 'midwifery'. She looked at me as though I was slightly deranged. The piece was never printed, so I took that to mean that her editor agreed with her.

The problem is widespread. Family doctors and their surgery staff are increasingly at the mercy of violent patients who abuse them verbally and physically. Aggressive behaviour by patients or their families is becoming an increasingly common feature of life in general practice. Recent surveys in London and the West Midlands show that more than half of all doctors have been verbally abused. The problem is at its worst in inner cities – 1 in 10 inner London doctors have been physically attacked in the last two years – but suburban and rural practices are not immune. And these statistics do not take into account other staff who are in the front line – the receptionist and the practice nurse. According to the General Medical Services Committee (1994) in their guidelines *Combating Violence in General Practice*:

> This unacceptable behaviour does not have to be tolerated. If doctors fail to take decisive action in the face of actual or threatened violence, they not only do a disservice to themselves, their staff and other colleagues, but they put at risk the mutual trust on which primary care is based. To tolerate abusive or violent behaviour invites the perpetrator to repeat his or her actions. Therefore, the prevention of violent or threatening behaviour is vital to our professionalism.

The problem of aggression and violence at work is not one of gender. The Trust's research shows that 7 out of 10 incidents at work are perpetrated on men. Outside the workplace the majority of assaults and attacks are also on men (for example, 83 per cent of attacks on London Underground are by young men on young men). Most attacks on women are in the home or in a place that is known to them, by people they know, or think they know. Women are in fact very good at defusing and avoiding aggression, verbal as well as physical. Men can often respond to aggression with aggression leading to confrontation, which can end in even more problems.

It is in the interest of employers – not only employees – to reduce violence at work. For employers, violence can lead to low morale and a poor image for the organization, making it difficult to recruit and retain staff. It can also mean extra costs, with absenteeism, higher insurance premiums and compensation payments. PTS (Post-Trauma Syndrome) is now a well-documented and recognized condition which can severely affect the way employees can continue to work, and may result in the need for skilled professional counselling. What is less obvious is that employees suffering such aggression as continuous verbal abuse can suffer considerably from stress-related problems. Quite simply, no employer can afford to turn a blind eye. All employers have a legal duty under Section 2(1) of the Health and Safety at Work etc. Act 1974 to ensure, so far as is reasonably practicable, the health, safety and welfare at work of their employees. This duty extends to protecting employees from violence.

Risk assessment is also an employer's explicit duty under the Management of Health and Safety at Work Regulations 1992. These regulations require that employers undertake a systematic general examination of their work activity and, if there are five or more employees, they must record the significant findings of that assessment. Under these regulations employers need to follow up their risk assessment with appropriate preventative and protective measures and management arrangements (for example, planning, organization, control, monitoring and review). They must give employees adequate information and training to be able to understand the risks and the measures (including procedures, policies etc.) taken to deal with them. Once these have been tried and agreed in consultation with employees and, whenever possible, their union representatives, it is then the employees' responsibility not to put themselves in danger, or their colleagues, or their workplace. Employees who deliberately ignore the procedures and policies for health and safety might be considered negligent should an incident occur. They must also report incidents, problems and shortcomings in arrangements to control risks.

The Trust has been working closely with the Loss Prevention Council on this issue. They are treating it as a serious concern and are urging insurance companies to pass on the message to employers that workplace violence (as described above) should be integrated with their health and safety responsibilities. If employers continue to suffer incidents without any sign of action they will certainly face scrutiny from Health and Safety regulators and perhaps from their employee's legal advisers. Under the revised CICB compensation it is certain that more employees will begin to sue employers should there be personal safety problems. The Trust has published guidelines for both employers and employees which have been contributed to and endorsed by both the CBI and the TUC.

In the Trust's experience, training, knowledge and understanding help to dispel fears. These benefits enable you to be better equipped to avoid an incident or to respond and cope afterwards should one occur.

Pauline Bibby proved to be the perfect choice for writing *Personal Safety for Social Workers* for the Trust (also published by Arena), so we were not surprised when she produced this quite excellent 'bible' on personal safety for the multi-disciplined workers in health care. It is packed with information which is really helpful in practice. It is easy to understand, enjoyable, and to the point. No one in health care can fail to empathize with the situations.

Dr Jane Fraser, who is both a doctor and journalist, read and contributed to the script for which we are most grateful. She said: 'I thought this was a really interesting and informative manuscript.' My own doctor's practice in Barnes read a copy of the draft text too. Dr Shelagh Olney's comments were:

> Your excellent text was given to me several weeks ago and I made several comments along the way, but realise now that these completely concur with those made by other medics, namely:
>
> 1 That we as a group tend to be excessively confident about our own safety in all situations whether threatening or not.
> 2 As a group we tend to blame ourselves for violent situations; we somehow believe that we are the antagonists.
> 3 We believe that violence results from the patient's illness, or a relative's anxiety.
>
> As health care workers, I firmly believe that we have a need to be 'loved' by our patients and hence any violence aimed at us tends to be under-reported.
>
> I have learnt a great deal from the text – I for one shall be much more careful in future. Thank you. I wish the book every success and look forward to seeing it on the shelves.

I echo those sentiments – this book may be a sign of our times. However, it provides positive and healthy guidelines for those who are dedicated to relieving pain, suffering and giving essential help in this most unruly world.

Diana Lamplugh OBE
Director, The Suzy Lamplugh Trust
March 1995

Introduction

There is a sad irony in the recognition that people whose work involves the care of others may find themselves attacked by the very people to whom they are offering a service. There is now, however, a growing body of evidence about violence against health care workers, with patients, their families and members of the general public all playing their part. Reports of violence have grown over recent years and there has been increasing concern about violence in health care settings.

Some of the incidents have attracted media publicity because of their serious nature, but it should be remembered that, for every incident resulting in serious injury or even death, there are many which have less immediate impact; their long-term effects, however, can be extremely damaging. Abuse and violence have a demoralizing and debilitating effect on staff, and apparently minor incidents can easily escalate into more dangerous situations if they are not properly managed.

Those working in primary and secondary health care settings all face special risks as they go about their work, and their employers have legal as well as moral responsibilities to deal with workplace safety. General practitioners, community nurses, midwives and health visitors can experience abuse or violence as they visit patients at home – sometimes from the general public, and sometimes from patients or their families. In GP surgeries, health centres and community clinics, the risks are shared with reception and administrative staff and with practice nurses and other health care workers. In hospitals, medical and reception staff, administrative personnel, security and domestic staff all have special needs in relation to safeguarding personal safety.

This book is produced in response to current concern about the safety of health care workers as they go about their professional tasks, and it deals with the issues which employers, managers and staff in health care

1

organizations need to address. It draws heavily on the work of Chris Cardy in association with Diana Lamplugh for The Suzy Lamplugh Trust on workplace safety[1] and incorporates additional material of particular significance to the delivery of health care. It is a companion volume to *Personal Safety for Social Workers*.[2]

Reported incidents of violence underline the need to adopt an organizational or team approach to preventing violence in the workplace. It only needs one member of a team to neglect simple safety procedures for that individual, and perhaps their colleagues, to be placed at risk. For this reason, a collaborative approach involving all team members, support staff and managers is needed to ensure a safe working environment.

Recognition of the risks which health care workers can routinely face has been slow, and some employers have adopted a reactive stance, only taking action after violent incidents have occurred. They can thus find themselves charged with failing in their statutory duties towards their employees, and having to make policy at a time of crisis. Support to staff who have been attacked has been patchy, and in some instances sadly lacking. The absence of explicit and well-understood procedures for dealing with violent attacks can leave the staff concerned feeling unsupported, anxious and stressed.

Health care workers, in their turn, may have experienced feelings of guilt when they have been unable to prevent aggression or assault. Senior medical personnel can feel embarrassed and afraid of accusations of inadequate performance or even negligence. More junior staff may lack confidence in the level of understanding and support their line managers will show, and they may feel that they will be blamed for the incident. As a result there is a tendency towards under-reporting of violent acts.

Nevertheless, there is growing awareness of the problem, and an acknowledged need to search for ways of dealing with workplace violence. A number of employing organizations have begun to address personal safety issues, developing policies to prevent and deal with violence and to protect their staff. Helpful guidance has, for example, been produced by the National Association of Health Authorities and Trusts (NAHAT).[3]

Personal Safety for Health Care Workers draws on established good practice to guide those agencies who are still developing policy and practice. It is also intended to help agencies in reviewing their existing personal safety strategies.

Part 1 reviews some of the information now available about violence in health care settings and within the context of violence in society at large. The respective roles and responsibilities of employers and employees are discussed, and guidance offered on developing a workplace personal safety policy and on the steps which will need to be taken for effective implementation. Advice is given on developing procedures for reporting violent incidents and for providing after-care to staff who have been on the receiving end of violence. This section also looks at the ways in which the design and management of the workplace can enhance personal safety, and provides guidelines to individual workers on the issues to consider when working away from their normal work base.

Part 2 contains detailed personal safety guidelines for use by individual staff in a variety of work situations. Their use will help workers to develop confidence, and to take simple precautionary measures as a matter of course.

Part 3 addresses training issues and provides a number of sample training programmes and handouts. It is not intended to teach experienced trainers how to do their job, but to provide guidelines as reminders or triggers for action in key areas, for example where the trainer is:

- relatively new to training, or inexperienced;
- new to this potentially sensitive subject, which can arouse personal or emotional responses;
- unused to training which has wider organizational and policy implications within the workplace, as well as implications for individual performance;
- new to the content, and wishing to concentrate on that while using the checklists to ensure attention is paid to all parts of the process;
- working with a co-trainer, when the checklists can be used to ensure there is an understood and agreed process throughout for which the individual trainers take responsibility.

The sample training programmes, or 'tasks', are designed to show the ways in which Part 1 can be used, and the types of training events which can be provided. Some trainers may be able to use them almost unchanged, but many will want to adapt or amend them significantly. In other cases trainers could simply lift the exercises and activities from various programmes to construct something to meet their own specific needs.

The select bibliography contains references and information about further reading, training resources lists, and other training materials, including videos, and sources of further help, advice and information can be found in the list of useful organizations.

The message of this book is that prevention is better than cure – proper attention to risk can reduce both the incidence of aggression and its development into violent acts. In many instances preventive action can have the dual effect of protecting staff, and also of providing quality health care services in a more sensitive way. Good practice implies a responsibility to ensure that health care, whether at primary or secondary level, can be delivered in conditions of safety for staff and patients alike.

References

1 Cardy, C. and Lamplugh, D. (1992), *Training for Personal Safety in the Workplace*, Aldershot: Connaught Training.
2 Bibby, P. (1994), *Personal Safety for Social Workers*, Aldershot: Arena.
3 National Association of Health Authorities and Trusts (1992), *NHS Security Manual*, Birmingham: NAHAT.

Part 1

Background

1 Violence at work

Attacks on health care workers form part of a more general pattern of incidents of workplace violence ranging from verbal abuse and harassment to assault causing death. This chapter considers that wider context and the development of what has been called a culture of violence within society.

Whilst there is growing awareness of the problem of violence, it is not clear to what extent violent incidents have actually increased, and what part has been played by greater awareness and a willingness to report such incidents.

Over the past 10–15 years there has been growing awareness of the problems posed by violence and aggression in the workplace and in work-related situations. There have been a number of highly publicized incidents involving people who have been attacked in the course of their work. These have included teachers, social workers, estate agents, bank and building society staff as well as health service professionals.

The roots of violence are multi-causal, with the demands of modern life having their impact on frustration levels. The current recession, for example, has brought its own pressures. Threatened work closures, reduced budgets and redundancies affect not only those directly involved, but also their families, friends and daily contacts in a variety of situations. Poor housing and difficult working conditions and hours all have their part to play: feelings of insecurity, frustration and loss of control increase personal stress. This in turn can lead to lack of objectivity and oversensitivity. When fear, pain or anxiety about health are added to this dangerous cocktail of pressures, it is all too easy for minor frustration to escalate into anger, and aggression to lead to acts of violence.

It is important for employers and staff to learn from violent incidents. All employers have a legal duty under Section 2(1) of the Health and Safety at Work Act 1974 to ensure, so far as is reasonably practicable, the health, safety and welfare at work of their employees. However, the benefits of developing an effective policy for preventing and dealing with violence at work extend far beyond any statutory requirements. Staff who are properly trained, confident and well-supported are better prepared to handle difficult situations, and are likely to be more effective in carrying out their work.

Strategies are needed to protect staff, and to reduce the likelihood of aggression developing into overt violence. Failure to develop a strategy to deal with violence at work can lead to litigation and negative publicity, compensation costs and higher insurance premiums. Some of the less obvious but very real costs arising from emotional stress are high sickness levels, absenteeism, high staff turnover, and reduced job satisfaction and morale. In turn these factors can contribute to difficulties in recruiting and retaining staff.

Physical attacks are clearly dangerous and can result in injury, disability, or even death. They also cause stress and anxiety. Similarly, serious or persistent verbal abuse and threats affect both individual effectiveness and personal morale. The costs of failure to address violence at work, and the personal, monetary and organizational benefits of effective action to combat violence, cannot be underestimated.

Employers face the challenge of developing policies and procedures which minimize the occurrence of violence, and providing measures for handling violent incidents which do arise.

The key to a successful strategy lies in an integrated approach by employers, trade unions and staff. Thus, a clear organizational policy statement on personal safety at work must be backed by awareness-raising at all levels, attention to the ways in which the setting itself can be adapted or better managed to reduce risk, training for managers and staff, and agreeing appropriate methods for responding to violent incidents and providing support to the staff involved.

Research by Phillips, Stockdale and Joeman for the Suzy Lamplugh Trust with the London School of Economics[1] concluded that:

- Violence at work is an issue for both employers and employees.
- It is widespread – not confined to 'women's work' or to the UK.
- Perceptions of risk do not always match reality.
- Anxiety is no substitute for action. Institutional provision is crucial to employees' safety – all too often action only follows a serious incident.
- Violence at work has high costs to both the individual and the organization.
- Young males are the group most vulnerable to physical attack in the course of work.

Some practical perspectives have emerged:

- Aggression and violence in the workplace is a people problem, not a gender problem – at least twice as many men as women suffer from assaults every year (and men are much less likely to report them).
- If women's needs are seen to be special as far as violence and aggression are concerned, it is likely that men will ignore their own problems with aggression as well as their attitudes and needs. They will continue to think of women as inferiors, instead of equal though different. Many of the external problems will go unchallenged.
- It must be assumed that men and women have equal but different problems with aggression and violence. They need to be allowed to tackle those problems without stigma, condemnation or surprise.
- Violence is not defined as solely assault, attack and rape – verbal abuse, sexual and racial harassment, bullying, innuendo and even deliberate silence can be the triggers which escalate a situation into something worse.
- Even if escalation does not take place and there is no overt aggression, most people are so badly affected by covert aggression that they feel, and therefore become, more vulnerable. Fear is very debilitating and can result in behaviour which signals vulnerability – muggers mug 'push-overs', that is, easy targets (once again men under-report).
- The majority of incidents of aggression or violence occur when people are out and about: at work, travelling to or from work, or during their personal lives. The most likely timing is late afternoon when the schools come out and the pubs close! Once again most attacks involve men aged 16–25. Eighty-five per cent of muggings on the London Underground are perpetrated by men on men.[2] Most attacks on women are by people they know. Most rapes occur in the home or on first dates.
- If remedial action is to be really effective, procedures, physical danger points and structural changes need to be considered by both employer and employee.

The implications of violence and the fear of violence are far-reaching. They impact on the ability of individuals and teams to carry out their professional duties. In 1991 a Department of Health review of findings from child death inquiries suggested the level of protection given to children may be affected by violence to social work staff by parents.[3]

Where threats have been made against social workers or against health care professionals, and especially where a parent has a history of violent behaviour, it is hardly surprising if the worker is fearful. The ability to share such fears, so that ways can be found of managing the situation, will be dependent on the worker feeling confident that supervisors and managers will respond in a supportive and helpful manner. Fear of violence can have a profound effect on the workers' personal lives.

The following chapters outline workplace safety issues and deal with those which are of particular relevance within health care settings, providing a systematic approach to developing personal safety strategies.

References

1   Phillips, C.M., Stockdale, J.E. and Joeman, L.M. (1989), *The Risks of Going to Work*, London: Suzy Lamplugh Trust.
2   Income Data Services (1990), *Violence Against Staff*, London: IDS Study 458.
3   Department of Health (1991), *Child Abuse – A study of enquiry reports 1980–1989*, London: HMSO.

2 The risks in perspective

The high-profile reporting of incidents of violence and the increased awareness of employers and employees of the risks at work have both positive and negative effects. On the one hand we all need to be aware of risks inherent in our life and work if we are to develop safe practices, but such knowledge and awareness can engender fear of violence that is out of all proportion to the risk. In assessing the risks we face we need to consider evidence from a range of sources, as well as look critically at our own working environment and practices, if we are to have a balanced view.

Research findings

In the 1980s the rise in the number of reported assaults of various kinds on employees in the course of their work outpaced the growth in violent crime in general. During the same period a series of publications based on the work of a variety of organizations and on research work served as evidence that violence at work was a growing source of concern. Employers' organizations, trade unions, professional bodies and others were all becoming increasingly aware of the problems of violence, and the need to prevent them wherever possible and deal with them effectively when they occur.

There is a general view that violence at work has been increasing. However, this is difficult to prove or disprove since there has been an absence of large-scale systematic record-keeping, and increases in recorded attacks could stem from the fact that reporting incidents has become more acceptable, rather than reflect an increase in violence.

The lack of data also makes it difficult to quantify either the levels of violence or any changes or differences from year to year, geographically or in particular occupational groups. Despite these limitations, the following pieces of work have contributed to a growing understanding of the nature, scale and effects of violence at work:

- In 1987 the Health and Safety Executive's Health Service Advisory Committee produced a report[1] which suggested that violence to health service staff was far more common than previously believed. In some areas of work violence to staff was a regular occurrence. A survey of 3 000 health service workers showed that in the previous year:
  - 0.5 per cent had an injury requiring medical assistance;
  - 11 per cent had a minor injury requiring first aid;
  - 5 per cent had been threatened with a weapon;
  - 18 per cent had been threatened verbally.

- The TUC's report on *Violence to Staff*[2] in 1988 highlighted the lack of a comprehensive body of data on violence at work. It then reviewed current initiatives on violence to staff in a range of employment sectors, and showed that awareness of the problem had increased but the nature and extent of the risks to employees was still unclear.
- The 1988 report of the Department of Health and Social Security Advisory Committee on *Violence to Staff*[3] concluded that the issue should be considered in the wider context of service provision and against the legal background of the Health and Safety at Work Act 1974. The report made recommendations for all DHSS services and argued that central strategies alone are insufficient; initiatives must take into account local circumstances. Where strategies for combating violence have not been developed the report proposed urgent action, even in certain services or areas where violence is not perceived as a problem. The report's principal recommendations were:
  - the development of local strategies which contain an assessment of the problem of violence;
  - preventive measures;
  - suitable responses;
  - support to staff who are victims of violence;
  - the importance of training in translating strategies into practical advice.

- In 1988 the *British Crime Survey (BCS)*[4] found that teachers, welfare workers and nurses are three times more likely than the average employee to be verbally abused or threatened. Other occupational groups with a similarly increased risk of abuse include managers in the entertainment sector, transport workers, male security guards and librarians.

- Phillips, Stockdale and Joeman[5] found that:

  - 8 per cent of people are likely to suffer an assault on their journey to or from work;
  - 20 per cent are likely to experience an unpleasant incident on their journey;
  - 20 per cent face threatening behaviour;
  - sexual harassment occurs most frequently, with 20 per cent of victims being women in professional occupations where they spend a substantial amount of time away from a base, or workers in shops and offices;
  - the frequency of physical attacks ranges from a relatively low 4 per cent for female office workers to approximately 15 per cent for male professionals who often work away from the office;
  - the incidence of experiencing threatening behaviour varies from 10 per cent among office-based professionals to 33 per cent for those who often meet clients.

- The *British Crime Survey* for 1988 showed that 25 per cent of crime victims said that the incident had happened at, or because of, work. Fourteen per cent of respondents said they had been verbally abused at work at least once in the previous year, and approximately 33 per cent of all threats of violence were received at work.

- Research published in 1987 by the Labour Research Department[6] was largely concerned with public services and showed that:

  - 98 per cent of workplaces had experienced instances of abuse or harassment;
  - 85 per cent of workplaces reported that threats of violence had been made;
  - 62 per cent of workplaces suffered one or more instances of actual violence, including 80 per cent of transport companies and 77 per cent of health authorities;
  - 28 per cent of workplaces had experienced violence using a weapon.

  In the survey of 210 workplaces with a total of over 86 000 employees, 67 per cent felt that the level of abuse and violence had increased during the past five years.

- The IDS Study 458 (May 1990) found that transport and hospital staff in particular are especially at risk late at night and at weekends. Hospital casualty departments find that the vast majority of assaults are clustered late on Friday and Saturday nights, when they are busiest.

- A West Midlands Survey in 1994[7] found that:
  - 63 per cent of GPs had suffered abuse;

- – 27 per cent had changed their work practice;
- – 12 per cent had struck off one or more patients because of fear of violence;
- – 11 per cent discussed aggression at practice meetings;
- – 9 per cent had installed panic buttons;
- – 7 per cent used deputizing services because of fear.

● The *Which? Report on Street Crime*[8] used the British Crime Survey as its basis because of the belief that it was a better indicator of crime rates than police statistics. The BCS figures show that:

- – the likelihood of being mugged, even in a high-risk area, is less than the 20 per cent chance of having a car or some of its contents stolen in a year;
- – mugging is more common in inner-city, multi-racial areas, council estates with low-income tenants and areas with 'non-family' housing (that is, from bed-sits to large detached properties);
- – men are more at risk from crime overall than women, and particularly from violent crime in the streets;
- – elderly people are less at risk from crime than young people, and not simply because they go out less. It is young men who are most at risk of assault and robbery;
- – Afro-Caribbean and Asian people are more likely to be the victims of crime than white people;
- – Asian people are more likely to suffer vandalism, personal theft and victimization by groups of strangers.

The risk of crime

While fear of crime is understandable – because of what we see and hear in the media, or because of having been subjected to violence or living in an area of high levels of crime – it is important to get the risks in perspective. In many cases the fear of crime is disproportionate to the actual risk. A Home Office study on *Fear of Crime*[9] shows that the perceived level of crime sometimes bears little resemblance to the true level, especially crimes of violence and sexual offences. People very often overestimate the risk of crimes of violence. Similarly, the proportion of all crimes that involve violence is generally overestimated.

The Home Office study and other similar work demonstrate that crimes of violence against the person represent only a small proportion of all crimes. The chance of an individual being a victim of violent crime is far less than the chance they have of being a victim of car crime. However, it is important to remember that:

- Even a small percentage of a total of 5.5 million crimes in general means there were 295 000 individual violent crimes in England and Wales in 1993.
- Although a crime may not involve violence against the person within the legal definition, it may still result in the individual feeling attacked and violated.
- Many incidents of violence at work go unreported in the workplace, let alone to the police.
- The crime statistics can only indicate the statistical probability of being a victim of violent crime; they do not take account of individuals at greater risk because of the work they do or the lifestyle they lead.
- Violent crime is not a gender issue in the way it is sometimes assumed to be, that is, that women are more at risk then men. In fact, many more subjects of violent crime are men than women. The majority of assaults are by young men on young men.

Sexual offences

In the year to June 1993 the police in England and Wales recorded 29 618 sexual offences, 0.5 per cent of the total of all crimes. This figure represented

Table 2.1   Breakdown of sexual offences by category

Offence	%
Buggery	4.0
Indecent assault on a male	10.5
Indecency between males	2.5
Rape	14.5
Unlawful sexual intercourse	6.1
Indecent assault on a female	55.5
Incest	1.2
Procuration	0.5
Abduction	1.1
Bigamy	0.3
Gross indecency with a child	3.9
Source: Home Office Research and Statistics Department (1993), London: HMSO.	

a fall in the number of offences of 125 over the previous twelve months' recorded sexual offences. Table 2.1 shows the figures for the different categories of sexual offences as a percentage of the total of all sexual offences.

More recent figures published in April 1994 do, however, show a 6 per cent increase in reported sexual offences to 31 400. Greater willingness to report such offences may be contributing to this increase in numbers.

As well as crime figures, other statistical information helps to put the risk of becoming the subject of a sexual offence into perspective. For example:

- About 40 per cent of rapes take place between people already known to each other.
- Over 60 per cent of rapes take place in buildings, homes or offices, rather than in the dark alleys we hear of in the more sensational press.
- Sexual offences against males are far more common than most people believe.
- You are more likely to become a rape victim between the ages of 16 and 24, and least likely under 10 years of age or over 60.
- The majority of convicted rapists are men in their twenties.
- Contrary to popular belief about night-time risks, many assaults and attacks take place in the afternoon after public houses close and children leave school.
- Statistically, any individual's chance of becoming a victim of a sexual offence is low, but other factors such as lifestyle, geographical location and occupation can change the probability.

Information of this sort can help in allaying unnecessary fears while enabling people to recognize real risks and thereafter make sensible judgements that will help to keep them safe. For example:

- Women should not assume that they are safe because they are meeting a man they know through work, particularly if they will be on his premises.
- Men should not assume they are safe from sexual offences simply because they are men.

References

1   Health and Safety Executive, Health and Safety Advisory Committee (1987), *Violence to Staff in the Health Services*, London: HMSO.
2   Trades Union Congress (1988), *Violence to Staff*, London: TUC Report.
3   Department of Health and Social Security Advisory Committee on Violence to Staff (1988), *Violence to Staff*, London: HMSO.

4   Home Office Research and Statistics Department (1988), *British Crime Survey*, London: HMSO.
5   Phillips, C.M., Stockdale, J.E. and Joeman, L.M. (1989), *The Risks of Going to Work*, London: Suzy Lamplugh Trust.
6   Labour Research Department (1987), *Assaults on Staff – Bargaining Report*, London: LRD, July.
7   Hobbs, R. (1994) 'General Practitioners' changes to practice due to aggression at work', *Family Practice*, Vol. II, No. 1, March.
8   Consumers' Association (1990), *Which? Report on Street Crime*, London: CA, November.
9   Home Office Public Relations Branch (1984), *Fear of Crime in England and Wales, Report of the Working Group*, London: Home Office Public Relations Branch.

3 Violence against health care workers

History

Whilst on the whole fears of violence may not be supported by evidence about violence in society, it is clear that certain occupations carry a special risk of violent attack. Information about violence in the health sector shows a disturbing pattern of threats and actual physical assaults.

Over recent years there have been a number of tragic incidents resulting in the deaths of health care workers as they went about their work which have highlighted the special risks faced by medical and related staff. In 1980 Carolyn Puckett, a health visitor for Oxford City Council, was killed by the father of a family she had been visiting. More recently, in September 1993, a man diagnosed as a paranoid schizophrenic with persecutory delusions, attacked and killed Georgina Robinson, a therapist, with a knife.

In a 1993 report on *Violence at Work*[1] Dr Vivienne Schneider and Ms Janet Maguire point out that 'violence is commonly encountered with the mentally ill, especially in hospitals'. The death in 1984 of social worker Isabel Schwarz who was stabbed by a mentally disturbed client on hospital premises, and the inquiry which eventually followed her death, underlined the growing concern about the safety of workers in hospitals.

Hospital accident and emergency departments are another problem area. In 1986 the Health Services Advisory Committee found that the areas most associated with violence were accident and emergency and psychiatric care.

These incidents have raised both professional and public awareness of the vulnerability to attack of workers in health care. A survey by *Doctor* magazine in 1992[2] found that of over 1 000 GP respondents, over 13 per cent had experienced actual physical attack, and that over 70 per cent had been threatened, verbally abused or attacked on a home visit.

GP surgeries are not immune from acts of violence. In February 1993 a woman GP was taken hostage at gunpoint by a middle-aged woman, and on another occasion a practice manager was threatened with a knife in an incident which lasted for several hours.

Incidence

While all the indicators are of growing violence and/or greater awareness and readiness to report violent incidents, the absence of uniform reporting and monitoring systems makes comparisons over time difficult and unreliable. A number of studies, however, have revealed higher than expected levels of violence against health care staff. They show that those attacks which have been highly publicized occurred against a background of widespread physical and verbal attacks on those responsible for some element of health care. Community nurses, for example, have described a wide range of abuse including the use of stones and bottles as missiles, verbal abuse, damage to cars, spitting and being followed.

These findings are disturbing not only because of the potential for minor incidents to escalate into serious assaults, but also because apparently minor incidents also provoke fear and anxiety; thus both health care workers and patients are adversely affected by a culture of threats and aggression.

Why?

Violence usually arises as a result of complex, inter-related factors. It is worth considering some of the possible reasons why medical and other health care staff are at special risk. They work daily with vulnerable people: many of the factors which contribute towards that vulnerability – for example illness, which may be combined with poverty, unemployment or family tensions – are factors which may well predispose those individuals towards violent or aggressive behaviour. In addition some patients may have a tendency towards temporary loss of control, for example because of alcohol or drug abuse while, where patients feel that they are not being kept fully informed, they can become angry and may use violence in an effort to gain control or to redress a perceived imbalance of power.

In a BBC radio programme broadcast in May 1994[3] Professor Richard Hobbs, professor of general practice at Birmingham University, noted that many of over 1000 GPs taking part in a West Midlands survey felt that patient anxiety was an important contributory factor in incidents of violence. It was also suggested during the programme that social mobility has a part to play. Where there is a highly mobile population and patients only register with GP practices for short periods, opportunities to develop relationships are very limited.

In hospitals, on the other hand, one obvious factor which may actually increase the risk of violence from a patient is the level of contact between patient and staff. Periods of hospital care provide opportunities for tensions to develop, and few natural breaks to allow for 'cooling down'.

Even when health care professionals have been aware of a patient's history of violence, reports from those who have been attacked indicate a sense of shock and surprise that the event had actually happened. There seems to be a denial by employees of the potential for violence against them, and it has been suggested that this denial develops to prevent workers becoming overwhelmed by fear, and thus feeling ineffective and powerless.

Unfortunately, this approach can also lead staff to underestimate or ignore the risk of attack, and to walk, ill-prepared, into very dangerous situations. Failure to anticipate the risk of violence, and lack of preparedness to deal with it, can in themselves contribute to the development of aggression into actual physical attack.

Victor Schwartz[4] describes the circumstances leading to the death of an American psychiatrist. The doctor was killed by a patient described as a chronic paranoid schizophrenic who had made repeated threats to kill his brother and had expressed hostility towards the psychiatrist:

> 'In hospital he threatened to shoot Dr O and a few others. One day, his aunt once again returned him to the hospital. He entered the reception area, put down his coat he was carrying over his arm, exposing a double-barrelled shotgun. He told the secretary he wanted to see Dr O. She went to his office and told him: "Mr F is out there with a shotgun. He says he wants to see you". Dr O rose from his desk and walked to the doorway, extending his hand as if to greet the returning Mr F. The patient fired the moment he entered the reception area and killed him instantly'.

This example illustrates the common case of the attacker making repeated and explicit threats, and the tendency to disregard these or underestimate their seriousness, with tragic results.

Changes in social policy, with an increasing emphasis on providing Care in the Community, mean that many people who previously lived in institutional settings because of their disturbed behaviour patterns now experience less restrictive care and treatment within community settings, or fall outside the care support net. Where properly planned community-based facilities are absent or inadequately resourced, then the ability to provide sensitive care and to secure the safety of health service staff becomes highly compromised.

In *Facing Physical Violence*[5] Breakwell makes the point that:

'If the health care services are understaffed and poorly resourced, then people working in them will face the frustration and anger of the ill and injured who are deprived of adequate provision'.

The combination of these factors – taken together with the opportunities for violence which occur in individual interviews and consultations – provide powerful arguments for the development and implementation of personal safety strategies for all who work in health care settings.

The effects of violence on staff

When a worker has been threatened or physically attacked, a number of responses are likely. Those who have experienced violence report initial 'freezing' at the moment of attack, closely followed by a sense of shock and surprise. Afterwards there is usually anger, which may be directed at the attacker, or at colleagues or the department in which they work.

There appears to be an unrealistic, and often self-imposed, expectation that health care workers, as professionals, should have been able to anticipate or prevent the attack, and this brings with it a sense of personal failure at not being able to do so. An assault, for example on a doctor, carrying out his or her responsibilities, is in effect a blow to both personal self-esteem and sense of professional competence.

Writing in *Community Care*,[4] Victor Schwarz argues that when a violent incident does occur it reflects the nature of modern society, and is not an indictment of a caring professional. Those working in medical and related professions need to be encouraged to make a careful and rational assessment of a patient's dangerousness, particularly where there have been serious and repeated threats.

It seems to be a reasonable assumption that people who work in the health service are concerned to help others, and they may well have difficulty in reconciling this with clear evidence that the patient views the worker as unhelpful or controlling. Some of those attacked report feelings of guilt at 'allowing it to happen' and at the subsequent prosecution by the police of the attacker.

The effects of a violent attack can include nausea, headaches, sleeplessness, shakiness and extreme fatigue, as well as the direct physical injuries sustained. The emotional and psychological impact of violence can be profound and long-term. Common responses include a sense of isolation and problems with decision-making in both the personal and professional areas of life.

Fear, anger and feelings of revenge, sadness, betrayal and self-doubt all play their part, with one or more of these being more evident at any one time. The fear of further violence, and lack of confidence in handling potentially violent individuals, can have a serious impact on professional practice. Sudden and unexpected feelings of overwhelming fear are not uncommon.

In *Community Care*[6] a senior social worker who received stab wounds to her hand and upper arm, reported that '[my] emotional injuries were much greater and affected many areas of my life, family, friends and my work'. Strategies to provide helpful after-care following acts of violence will need to take account of the impact of violence on the workers concerned, and on their colleagues. They should also recognize that individuals will vary in their responses.

References

1   Schneider, V. and Maguire, J. (1993), *Violence at Work and its Impact on the Medical Profession Within Hospitals and the Community*, London: British Medical Association, September.
2   *Doctor* magazine (1992), Vol. 12, No. 19, 5 November.
3   British Broadcasting Corporation, 'File on 4', programme no. 94 VY3020NHO, transmitted 17 May 1994.
4   Schwartz, V. (1987), 'Social worker heal thyself', *Community Care*, 8 January, pp. 14–15.
5   Breakwell, G.M. (1989), *Facing Physical Violence*, London Psychological Society and Routledge.
6   Stevens, J. (1988), 'Healing the hidden wounds', *Community Care*, 8 September, pp. 22–3.

4 Defining violence and aggression

The first step in developing a personal safety strategy is for the organization to produce working definitions to clarify just what it is that is being addressed. Violence and aggression are often spoken of as if it is perfectly clear what they are, and indeed the two terms are often used interchangeably. Individual perceptions of violence and aggression differ, however. It is all too easy to assume that there is some shared, readily understood concept of such behaviour, as well as common knowledge of the scale of violence and aggression at work and elsewhere.

Just as perceptions of violence vary, so too do reactions. Some staff do not acknowledge violence as a problem in their job, while others may be anxious to the extent of being unable to carry out their professional tasks effectively.

Dictionary definitions focus on the words and what they mean in an objective, academic sense. They tell us something of what is generally understood by the terms 'violence' and 'aggression'. Such definitions do not, however, touch on the causes or effects of aggression and violence, nor how to recognize either of these in an organizational or work context.

There have been attempts to produce 'working' definitions, and these generally seek to describe the behavioural characteristics associated with aggression and violence and their effects. Some examples of 'working' definitions are:

- 'Any incident in which an employee is abused, threatened or assaulted by a member of the public in circumstances arising out of the course of his or her employment.' (Health and Safety Executive's working definition of violence, 1988)[1]
- 'The application of force, severe threat or serious abuse by members of the public towards people arising out of the course of their work whether or not they are on duty. This includes severe verbal abuse or

25

threat where this is judged likely to turn into actual violence; serious or persistent harassment (including racial or sexual harassment); threat with a weapon; major or minor injuries; fatalities.'[2]

● 'Behaviour which produces damaging or hurtful effects, physically or emotionally, on people.'[3]

These working definitions widen the dictionary definitions to encompass verbal aggression or abuse, threat or harassment. They also attempt to describe the behaviour associated with aggression and violence as well as its effects on the person attacked. Although some working definitions deal specifically with behaviour from the public, most are wide enough to take into account that 'the public' would include contact with other agencies, contractors, service providers and others with whom an organization does business. In addition, although not directly mentioned, there remains the possibility of aggressive or violent behaviour from colleagues within the workplace.

Seeking a definition may seem rather pedantic but it is an important, although often forgotten, basic step in addressing problems of aggression and violence at work, for these reasons:

● We need to know what it is we are talking about and trying to manage. Many people still assume violence only includes serious physical attack, rape and murder. In practice a wide range of behaviour is now recognized as violent or aggressive and appreciated as being damaging to individual employees and the work of the organization. The range of behaviour includes:

Physical violence	**Non-physical violence**
– assault causing death	– verbal abuse
– assault causing serious physical injury	– racial or sexual abuse
– minor injuries	– threats – with or without weapons
– kicking	– physical posturing
– biting	– threatening gestures
– punching	– abusive 'phone calls
– use of weapons	– threatening use of dogs
– use of missiles	– harassment in all forms
– spitting	– swearing
– scratching	– shouting
– sexual assault	– name-calling
– deliberate self-harm	– bullying
	– insults
	– innuendo
	– deliberate silence.

- Developing a definition should take into account the context and culture of the organization and the characteristics of the staff and the potential aggressors. For example:
  - a mentally ill person may not be capable of making rational judgements about behaviour and could lash out verbally or physically;
  - people in places of entertainment or pubs may swear as a result of high spirits and alcohol in some cases, but present no threat.

  Considering the contextual issues in developing a definition helps to ensure that it is workable because it encompasses what the organization (employers and employees) believes to be violent behaviour, as opposed to behaviour resulting from other factors.
- Perceptions of aggression and violence will vary between those who have experienced violence and those who have not, and between people at high risk and people at much less risk. Not everyone will be equally vulnerable or resilient when it comes to dealing with violence or the fear of it. A process of involving people in working towards a definition brings a variety of experiences, views and perceptions into the open so that they can be taken into account in developing a definition to which everyone can subscribe. Thus it is important to involve locally-based and centrally-based staff, as well as professional associations and trade unions in arriving at agreed working definitions.
- A definition, although artificial in some ways, can be shared, explained and understood, thereby establishing a basis for recognizing violence as such. General understanding can significantly increase people's willingness to report incidents. Under-reporting of incidents has been a serious problem that many believe results from a lack of confidence that reports of violence will be perceived by others as the person attacked perceives them. The dismissing of reports as 'part of the job' or the oversensitivity of the employee has been all too common.

Developing a working definition of aggression and violence for the organization is therefore an important foundation of understanding upon which to build commitment, policy, procedures and working practices.

It does not matter if someone else's definition is used as a starting point, or the process is begun with a blank sheet of paper. Whether aggressive behaviour and violent behaviour are defined separately, or 'violence' is used as a term to cover a continuum of behaviour (as many organizations do), is not critical. Nor does it matter whether the definition sounds learned or is simply a straightforward list of behaviour. What does matter is that the definition is developed in such a way that it is shared and so can inform the future behaviour and perceptions of everyone. This implies consultation with the workforce, specifically those people most likely to be at risk, rather than the imposition of a definition by policy-makers, managers or others relatively remote from the 'front line'. This may appear a long-winded and time-consuming way of arriving at a form of words, but it is well worth doing as it can cover a good deal of the groundwork necessary to develop a policy (see Chapter 7).

So far as this book is concerned, 'violence' is used as an all-embracing term and is defined as:

> 'any behaviour towards an employee in the course of his or her work that has damaging physical or psychological effects upon the person'.

This definition includes all forms of physical and non-physical abuse, attack, threat or assault, and is intended to be victim-centred in that the assessment of what is damaging, particularly psychologically, must come from the subject of violence himself or herself.

Throughout the remainder of this book the use of the term 'victim' of violence has been kept to a minimum. It is important to avoid any tendency to stigmatize those who have been on the receiving end of violence and aggression. Rather, the focus needs to be on helping employers to take responsibility for the problem and for seeing that staff are positively supported in dealing with issues of violence.

References

1   Health and Safety Executive (1988), *Preventing Violence to Staff*, London: HMSO.
2   Department of Health and Social Security Advisory Committee on Violence to Staff (1988), *Violence to Staff*, London: HMSO.
3   Association of Directors of Social Services (1987), *Guidelines and Recommendations to Employers on Violence against Employees in the Personal Social Services*, Worcester: ADSS.

5 Employer and employee roles

Section 2(1) of the Health and Safety at Work Act 1974 imposes a general obligation and specific applications of it upon employers. The general obligation is:

'it shall be the duty of every employer to ensure, so far as is reasonably practicable, the health, safety and welfare of all his employees'.

The matters to which that duty extends include:

- 'The provision and maintenance of plant and systems of work that are, so far as is reasonably practicable, safe and without risk to health.'
- 'The provision of such information, instruction, training and supervision as is necessary to ensure, so far as is reasonably practicable, the health and safety at work of his employees.'
- 'The provision and maintenance of a working environment for his employees that is, so far as is reasonably practicable, safe and without risk to health.'

In addition there is an obligation to draw up and publish written safety policies to include these matters. Apart from the obligations under the Health and Safety at Work Act, there are other obligations on an employer arising from:

- The employer's duty of care under Common Law for the safety of his or her employees.
- The employer's duty under any nationally negotiated agreements.
- The employer's duty not to dismiss employees unfairly. Employees have resigned in some situations and successfully alleged constructive unfair dismissal because the employer failed to provide reasonable precautions for the employee's safety, thus establishing a precedent.

Employers face penalties under the Health and Safety at Work Act if they fail to meet their obligations. Employees also have the option of seeking other remedies where any employer fails to fulfil his or her duty, including damages, industrial action and resignation followed by a claim for constructive unfair dismissal.

The key question arising from this is: 'What is meant by "reasonably practicable"?' The meaning is largely governed by case law, of which the most important case is a Court of Appeal case, *Edwards* v. *National Coal Board* [1949] IKB 704. In giving judgment, Lord Justice Asquith said:

> '"reasonably practicable" is a narrower term than "physically possible" and seems to me to imply that a computation must be made by the owner in which the quantum of risk is placed on one scale and the sacrifice involved in the measures necessary for averting the risk (whether in money, time or trouble) is placed in the other'.

The principles of this case would apply to proceedings under the Health and Safety at Work Act or any other similar kind of proceedings. This means that:

- the burden of proof that all reasonably practicable measures have been taken rests upon the employers;
- the employers must be able to show that they had applied their minds to the computation mentioned by Lord Justice Asquith;
- courts will decide on the factual evidence whether the employers are entitled to rely upon the 'reasonably practicable' defence.

These principles have been upheld in a number of cases arising from areas of employment as varied as local authorities, mining and the entertainment industry. In other cases the judges have made it clear that there is a requirement on employers to:

- take action to minimize risks to employees;
- take into account the risk of criminal attack as part of the obligation to provide a safe system of work.

The enforcement of the Health and Safety at Work Act can be:

- by an improvement notice, when an inspector considers health and safety legislation is being contravened;
- by a prohibition notice, when an inspector considers there is a risk of serious personal injury;
- by prosecution for breach of the Health and Safety at Work Act or its relevant statutory provisions.

A breach of Sections 2–6 of the Health and Safety at Work Act attracts a £20 000 fine; breach of other relevant statutory provisions £5 000. Magistrates may imprison for up to six months individuals who fail to comply with an improvement or prohibition notice; in the Crown Court the period is two years.

Another aspect of the Health and Safety at Work Act is sometimes forgotten, that is, the duty it places upon individuals. In Section 7 of the Act it is made clear that it is the

'duty of every employee to take reasonable care for the health and safety of himself and other people who may be affected by his acts or omissions at work'.

Of particular interest is Section 37, which shows that offences under the Act may be committed either by individual people or by corporate bodies such as limited companies, nationalized industries or local authorities. If an offence committed by a corporate body was committed with the consent or connivance of, or because of the negligence of, a director, manager, secretary or other officer, that party is also guilty of the offence, and may be prosecuted as well as the corporate body. Although prosecutions of individuals under this provision have been rare, it is well worth managers and others remembering its existence and the implications for them personally.

The balance struck within the Act between employer and employee responsibility is extremely important. It is pointless for an employer to develop safe working practices if members of the workforce do not observe the rules of safe working, fail to follow the procedures laid down or otherwise put themselves and/or others at risk – for example, through practical jokes or horseplay resulting in injury. Similarly an employee can strive to work safely but his/her ability to do so can be severely limited without the commitment and support of the employer.

Some of the general duties of the Health and Safety at Work Act have been supplemented by the Management of Health and Safety At Work Regulations 1992, which implement the EC Framework Directive on Health and Safety. The regulations require that employers undertake a systematic general examination of their work activities and record significant findings of their assessment. A risk assessment must identify:

- the extent and nature of the risk;
- the factors which contribute to the risk;
- the causes; and
- the changes necessary to eliminate or control the risk.

Clearly assessments will vary according to the type of work involved, location and working patterns. In looking at risk in the health care setting, consideration should be given to factors which affect the interaction between health professional and patient as well as the patient's family. Reviews should be at regular intervals and form part of standard management practice.

It is not only the statutory responsibility or other imposed obligations that provide the motivation to develop safe working practices. There are personal and organizational costs associated with violence in the workplace. Personal attack or injury can lead to staff absences on sick leave, as a result of the injury itself or because of psychological damage caused by it which leads to depression, insomnia, agoraphobia or panic attacks. The employer may face litigation costs or insurance claims which in turn lead to higher insurance costs, and an attack is likely to lead to bad publicity for the organization itself. In addition, employee effectiveness is likely to be reduced by loss of confidence, anxiety and stress, and may involve fear of certain aspects of work.

Any form of violence, whether or not it results in some sort of physical injury, can have serious adverse effects on the workforce, including:

- high levels of anxiety;
- stress-related illness;
- absenteeism and the need to cover for staff;
- low morale;
- high levels of staff turnover;
- low productivity;
- little job satisfaction;
- low employee involvement;
- industrial action or poor industrial relations;
- difficulty in recruiting and retaining staff.

So far as health services are concerned, there is an additional factor to be taken into account. By their very nature health care services are aimed at the prevention and alleviation of pain and distress; there is a responsibility on both employing agencies and individual workers to take notice of the risk of violence, and to develop a system which offers patients assistance in an organized and safe fashion in which both worker and patient can feel secure. Failure to do this, with resulting violence, is a reflection on the quality of care offered by the service.

In situations where there is an endemic problem of violence there is a tendency to accept it as part of the job. Medical personnel understand that patients may be anxious or stressed and may 'make allowances' for behaviour which others would consider unacceptable. Studies have found an unwillingness to report violent incidents to management, unions or the police, with a tendency to regard such occurrences as an occupational hazard. This is dangerous, both in the sense that it ignores a problem with potentially very serious consequences for individuals and the organization, and also because the tendency to dismiss the problem frequently comes from managers or others who are least likely to suffer directly from the problem.

Despite the clear duties and obligations placed on employers and employees, there are many workplaces with very limited arrangements for tackling the problem of violence at work. Some workplaces have no arrangements at all.

The Labour Research Department *Bargaining Report*[1] found that:

- only 45 per cent of the workplaces where actual violence had occurred had any system of monitoring violent incidents;
- 67 per cent felt that the level of violence/abuse had increased in recent years;
- only 31 per cent of workplaces had a management structure providing someone with overall responsibility for dealing with abuse/violence;
- 86 per cent of workplaces felt that their management should take more responsibility for the health and safety of staff exposed to risks of abuse/violence;
- despite the fact that 69 per cent of the workplaces surveyed had experienced actual violence, only 11 per cent had taken industrial action over the issue.

The Health and Safety Executive's booklet *Preventing Violence to Staff*[2] suggests that the best way to tackle violence in the workplace is for employers and employees to work together through an action plan.

The proposed action plan has the following seven steps, with the key points in each step identified.

- **Step 1: Find out if there is a problem**
  - It is easy for employers to think there is not a problem; employees may feel differently.
  - The easiest way to find out about problems is by asking staff, either informally or by using a formal method such as a questionnaire.
  - Communicate the result of any investigation to staff. If there is a problem they then know the employer recognizes it; if there is not a problem any unfounded fears will be put to rest.
  - If a survey does not identify a problem things could still change, so it is wise to check the situation from time to time.

- **Step 2: Record all incidents**
  - Keeping records helps build up a picture of the problem. A simple form can be used to gather the details needed – for example, what

happened, when, where and to whom.
- Employees may not be keen to report incidents if they accept violence as part of the job or feel reporting it will reflect badly on them; having a reporting system and communicating the fact that reports are needed to tackle the problem can encourage reporting.

- **Step 3: Classify all incidents**

  - The reporting system should classify all incidents so that details about the location, frequency, severity, nature and consequences of the incident can be gathered.
  - Classification can assist in identifying areas or types of work where particular problems occur, patterns of incidents and, in some cases, causes, and so help target any steps taken to tackle the problems.
  - The classification used will depend on needs. It is easy to classify fatal injury, major injury, physical injury requiring hospital treatment or first aid, and injury requiring time off work. It is less easy to classify incidents where the result is emotional shock, feelings of threat, or effects requiring counselling or time off work. Any classification should be understood by all those using it and should be used consistently.

- **Step 4: Search for preventive measures**

  - Finding appropriate preventive measures rarely means selecting off-the-shelf solutions to problems. The key is being clear about what the problem is and then devising ways of overcoming it that will work in particular circumstances.
  - Employees who perform the jobs where there are risks can be a good source of ideas, as can other similar organizations with procedures in place, health and safety specialists, the police or security advisers.
  - It is important that both employers and employees are open to solutions that require changes in procedures and working practices. Sometimes solutions may be perceived as less efficient but in the long term prove to be cost-effective.

- **Step 5: Decide what to do**

  - Employees are more likely to be committed to any measures that they themselves help to design and put into practice. Often trade union representatives and health and safety officers have experience in measures that can be taken.
  - A mix of measures can often work best by balancing the risks to employees with any possible side-effects of measures on the public or patients that could increase the potential for violence.

- **Step 6: Put measures into practice**
  - Whatever measures are decided on, the policy for dealing with violence should be included in the organization's health and safety policy statement so that all employees are aware of it. This will encourage cooperation in following procedures and reporting incidents.

- **Step 7: Check that measures work**
  - Once the preventive measures have been in place for a time it is important to check how well they are working.
  - There are various methods to help with assessment, such as comparing the number and types of incidents, the level of reporting of incidents, and changes in employees' feelings about the situation.
  - Often joint management and trade union committees are an effective means of monitoring the measures.
  - If the measures work, keep them up.
  - If the measures are not effective, reassessing the problems and finding alternative measures may be necessary.

Of course, these steps can be embodied in a policy – this is dealt with in Chapter 7.

References

1 Labour Research Department (1987), *Assaults on Staff – Bargaining Report*, London: LRD, July, pp. 5–12.
2 Health and Safety Executive (1988), *Preventing Violence to Staff*, London: HMSO.

6 Safety in the health care setting

Once it has been recognized that employers and employees both have a duty in respect of safe working practices, and that not combating violence at work has potentially serious costs, many organizations start to take positive steps to tackle the problems. A systematic approach will help to achieve a coherent policy backed by procedures for implementation.

Identifying the risks

The first step has to be that of identifying the risks. Most jobs still require people to get to and from a place of work, and there are risks associated with travelling; the premises in which people work can be susceptible to break-in, and almost no one works in such isolation that there is no risk from contacts – or even colleagues. Most health care settings are by their nature open and easily accessible to members of the general public.

Certain occupations are recognized as having a relatively higher risk of violence attached to them. The Health and Safety Executive[1] breaks these jobs into the following categories:

- 'Giving a service: benefits office, housing department;
- Caring: nurses, social workers, community care staff;
- Education: teachers, non-teaching staff;
- Money transactions: post offices, banks, shops, building societies, bus drivers/conductors;
- Delivery/collection: milk delivery, postal services, rent collection;
- Controlling: reception staff, security staff, traffic wardens;
- Inspecting: building inspectors, planning officers.'

Clearly staff working in health care fall into more than one of the above job categories. They provide a range of services in the hospitals and within the community, and their work includes some elements of control. They may work routinely with confused or demented patients, and may experience challenging behaviour from people with learning disabilities. They and their employing organization need to work together on a sensible, practical approach which will ensure that violence is monitored, managed and prevented.

All people who have direct contact with the general public in the course of their work should be aware of the need to avoid and prevent violence, and should be properly prepared to deal with incidents which do occur. In health care there is a special need to recognize that certain situations may carry a particular risk of violence. These situations will need to be carefully structured to reduce its likelihood. Some examples include:

- **Accident and emergency work:** Accident and emergency work carries with it high levels of risk. Attention should be given to staffing levels and the need to ensure that staff are not working in isolated circumstances.

- **Assessments for action under the Mental Health Act 1983:** Mental health assessments, and continuing work in the mental health field, have the potential to attract violence. Rowett found in his study[2] that the clients most likely to attack field social workers were those with a recognized mental illness.

- **Child protection work:** The decision to intervene in order to protect a child considered to be at risk of physical, sexual or emotional abuse represents a major invasion of family life. When parental capacity to care for and protect a child is called into question, it is hardly surprising that intervention, and in some cases removal of the child, will lead to feelings of anger, denial and guilt. GPs, health visitors and paediatric medical and nursing staff may well be seen as threatening, with attendant feelings of anger.

- **Transporting patients:** Particular attention is needed where patients are being transported, especially where an ambulance has been called to a scene of violence. Guidance on how to handle violence should be part of the basic training for all ambulance staff.

- **Home visits:** Health professionals who work in the community need to make a careful assessment of the risks involved, and to work out with colleagues how to deal with a situation where there is some threat. Joint visits are one way of dealing with potentially dangerous situations, but there is some evidence that the presence of additional people can actually increase the risk of violence. Each case will need to be considered in the light of the available knowledge.

In some areas community nurses and health visitors have discontinued the wearing of uniforms, feeling that such distinctive dress could mark them out as having access to drugs and possibly put them at risk of attack.

- **Out of hours visits:** A survey of GPs carried out by *Pulse* magazine[3] found that 10 per cent of the 500 GPs who took part reported assaults during daytime home visits and 10 per cent reported incidents occurring during night calls. In some areas arrangements have been made for doctors making night calls to use driver services with radio back-up, rather than drive alone to make their house calls.
- **Work with addiction:** Work in the fields of drug dependence, alcohol or substance abuse carries with it special risks associated with addictive behaviour and loss of control. An individual who is usually even-tempered can suffer sudden loss of control when using drugs or alcohol, or when deprived of access to them.

  Drug dependency brings with it the additional danger of addicts seeking access to controlled drugs or to prescription forms. Security arrangements which keep prescription forms out of sight, and drugs properly stored, will help to reduce risk.
- **Visiting new patients:** Any indication of previous aggression or physical violence, or factors which may predispose the patient to be violent, should be carefully recorded. Account will need to be taken of this information when making decisions on case allocation and management.

Training to raise staff awareness, and guidelines aimed at violence avoidance, have both tended to concentrate on the need for individuals to recognize potentially dangerous situations, and to act to defuse them. Too often the message appears to be that, where incidents do arise, the worker concerned is at fault. Whilst staff do need training in risk assessment and dealing with potential and actual violence, it is essential to acknowledge that no amount of training will provide universal protection. Nor is training alone the answer. To be effective, a safety strategy requires organizational acceptance of responsibility to work with staff on policy development, production of guidance, and training for all health care workers and their line managers.

Particular attention must be paid to situations such as those outlined above, where there is a recognizable additional danger. Staff need to feel confident that they can depend on management to be supportive and responsive to their needs. Any tendency to attribute blame, or to label those assaulted as provocative or unskilled, is likely to lead to unvoiced fears and unhelpful under-reporting.

GPs have a dual role to play in developing good personal safety practice.

They are both front-line workers in health care, facing risk from patients and their families, and also employers and managers of practice- and community-based staff with similar problems. They are, therefore, well placed to work with colleagues at reducing the risk and effects of violence at the surgery and in the home. In doing so, they should have the advice and support of Family Health Services Authorities on how to avoid violence at work.

A successful safety strategy requires a holistic approach which affects all areas of work and all levels of staff. It must be proactive, anticipating and dealing with areas of risk and taking measures to handle these; it must also be responsive, learning from experience and encouraging the open discussion and debate of safety policy and practice.

Conducting a personal safety audit

One way of finding out if there is a problem and identifying risks at work is to conduct an audit – a detailed, systematic, official investigation. An audit should look not only at *what* is done, but also *how* things are done; it is here where problems often arise. An audit must be an 'official' investigation: this implies organizational commitment to the exercise and an intention to act upon its findings. An audit will raise both awareness and expectations among employees, and it is therefore important that action on its findings does in fact follow.

Trying to investigate an organization as a whole could well be an impossible task, especially where it is large and has a number of sites or departments doing different types of work. Investigating site by site, or department by department, makes the task much more manageable. It helps to identify site- or department-specific issues, or problems associated with particular types of activity. Common issues can of course be identified and dealt with as such.

Areas which should be investigated include issues of access to places of work. It will be necessary to see what controls on access there are and whether staff have the means of summoning help. The extent to which staff work in isolated circumstances will also need to be reviewed, and account should be taken of any problems which have already arisen, and whether staff are concerned about working in isolation.

Reception arrangements should be looked at closely. In GP surgeries and health centres care should be taken that prescription forms are not accessible to patients and that unused syringes are not stored in open areas. Careful arrangements should be made for the disposal of used syringes. The general ambience of the area in which visitors are received should be reviewed. Is it welcoming and friendly, for example, as well as designed to control access and protect staff? Are people kept waiting or dealt with promptly? Is the workplace itself isolated? Is it well-lit? Are there problems associated with the storage and dispensing of drugs, and are there safer ways of dealing with this? Are there particular days and times when the incidence of violence is high? A 1985 study of violence in the accident and emergency department of Edinburgh Royal Infirmary[4] revealed that 37 per cent of incidents occurred between 22.00 hours and 02.00 hours.

Many health care workers are expected to work late or at night. It may be necessary to arrange safe transport for certain staff, or to review security in car parks, especially at night.

There is an additional factor to be taken into account when considering how best to reduce the incidence of violence. This relates to those circumstances in which professional health care is provided in secondary settings – for example, in residential or nursing homes, prisons or hostels. In these situations individual medical and nursing staff need to be well-informed about current safety procedures, and may need to involve senior managers in agreeing policy and practice with the 'host' setting.

An audit should consider the special problems which may be associated with work in secondary settings. It should also address the issue of how home visits are organized and recorded, and whether there are procedures for staff to call in if they feel at risk, change their plans or are delayed.

Many health care workers travel in the course of their work, and a review of travel arrangements should provide details of travel methods, arrangements for dealing with car breakdown, and any incidents of violence which have been experienced.

The safety audit should also consider who receives a service – either at home or in a surgery, clinic or hospital setting. People needing health care are often likely to be concerned, upset, annoyed or angry. Some may have a history of aggression.

It is important before embarking on an audit to be clear about the information needed. Establish whether the audit will deal with one or more departments and whether it is aimed at particular groups of staff, or employees who undertake particular tasks. It is helpful to collect information about staff feelings and attitudes towards the problem of violence at work, and about the level of awareness of staff in relation to safety procedures. Information will also be needed about actual incidents of violence.

Investigation methods   Some investigation methods involve the collection of 'hard' data – yes/no answers, numerical scores, choices from a checklist, and so on. Examples include the number of incidents of violence, the percentage of people feeling at risk, or rankings of what staff believe are the most dangerous situations. This sort of data is easy to collate and quantify.

Other methods generate information which is more difficult to quantify, but which can be helpful in forming a picture of staff views, opinions and anecdotal evidence. Descriptions of procedures used and individual views about how these might be improved fall within this category.

The simpler the information to be collected, the easier it will be to use. The key is to achieve a balance between simplicity and the collection of useful information. Remember that too much information can be difficult to handle effectively and that resources will be needed to analyse and present the audit findings. It is important at the outset to commit sufficient resources to handle the audit, and to set a realistic timescale for the exercise.

A simple, straightforward approach generates information that can be readily analysed and acted upon. It is well worth making time at the planning stage to do the groundwork thoroughly, as this will increase the chances of getting exactly what you need from the investigation in a form that is manageable, and will actually save time in the long run.

Methods of collecting information include the use of questionnaires, observation, structured interviews, working groups and the use of external consultants. Some more detailed guidance about these methods appears at the end of this chapter. This is not exhaustive, but provides a structure within which to plan your safety audit.

Other methods which have proved effective include:

● suggestion boxes;
● use of team meetings with supervisors or managers;
● staff meetings or departmental meetings;
● asking people to write in with views, ideas, problems, opinions, and so on;
● open forums with safety or personnel staff;
● visits to other workplaces to observe different practices.

It is necessary to remember that no method is perfect and will give precisely all the information sought. Whichever method or combination of methods is selected, people should be made aware of what is being done and why, and be involved whenever possible. The outcome of the audit exercise should also be made available as quickly as possible.

The organization may have staff with skills and experience in information collection and management. If it does not, or if staff are already fully stretched, then it may be necessary to seek external help in conducting an audit. Such a decision may reduce staff anxiety and encourage honesty and openness; management may also be more accepting of an external view of the findings. Where the decision is to conduct the audit in-house, an existing or specially-created joint management–staff group can be tasked with conducting the investigation. This is often regarded as the best option to secure contributions, cooperation and commitment to the process and its outcomes.

Finally, the findings should be acted upon as soon as practicable. There may well be risks which can be dealt with immediately, and these should be tackled, thus reassuring staff of the commitment to act. Other more complex problems may take time to deal with; where this is the case it is important to keep staff in touch with progress that is being made so that they know the problem is being tackled.

Some guidance on investigation methods

When selecting investigation methods it is wise to pause before making a choice, to answer some basic questions. This process will help in identifying an effective, acceptable and manageable method that will suit the particular circumstances.

What information do you want?

- Do you want information about the whole organization; one or more departments, or sections; groups of staff thought to be at risk, or employees who undertake particular jobs or tasks?
- Do you want to collect information about people's feelings and attitudes to the problem of violence at work; identify gaps in safety measures; test out the level of awareness of staff in relation to safety procedures, or collect data on actual incidents of violence?

What form of information do you want?

- Some methods generate so-called 'hard data': yes/no answers, numerical scores, choices from a list, ticks on a chart, and so on. These are data that can be quantified readily and information, such as percentages, derived from them.
- Other methods generate information which is much more difficult to quantify: views, opinions and anecdotal evidence are potentially infinitely variable because you do not put limits on the choice of responses to the questions, and everyone will answer in their own way.
- Do you want numerical information such as the number of incidents of violence, the percentage of people that feel at risk, or rankings of what employees believe are the most dangerous tasks?
- Do you want information in the form of descriptions of procedures used, anecdotal evidence of people's experiences of violent incidents or near misses, or, perhaps, individual views about what are unsafe practices and how they could be improved?
- The simpler the information you collect the easier it will be to use. How simple can you keep your investigation but still get the information you need?

How much information should you collect?

- There is often a tendency to collect as much information as possible in one process. However, how much of each type of information can you handle effectively? Will you have any help when it comes to analysing it? How experienced are you and others in analysing and presenting information? Collecting information you cannot use is a waste of time.
- What levels of commitment and resources are there in the organization? Collecting more information than can be acted upon because of lack of commitment or resources is also a waste of time. It may also raise expectations that cannot be fulfilled and thus create problems.
- What timescales are you working to, and what can realistically be achieved in that time?

Who should conduct the investigation?

- Who has skills or experience in information collection and management? Is external help a good idea and/or possible?
- If management conducts the investigation will staff feel able to be open and honest, critical if necessary or willing to admit a lack of understanding or confidence? Will the outcomes be accepted as reliable by everyone?
- If staff representatives investigate will management feel able to accept the findings without reservation?
- Could an existing, or created, joint management–staff group be responsible for conducting the investigation? This is often regarded as the best option to secure contributions, cooperation and commitment to the process and its outcomes.

An investigation does not have to be a complex or long-winded process; frequently the simple, straightforward approach generates information that can be readily analysed and acted upon. Like most things, the preparation for an investigation makes subsequent conduct and use of the information gathered very much easier. It is well worth making time at the planning stage to do the groundwork thoroughly as this will increase the chances of getting exactly what you need from the investigation, in a form that is manageable and will actually save time in the long run.

A few examples of methods of collecting information, with some guidelines on using them and points about them, follow.

Questionnaires

- Decide who is responsible for the investigation.

- Be quite clear about what information you want to collect so that the questionnaire can be constructed to do this.
- Keep it as simple as possible.
- Agree who will be involved in the construction, application and analysis of the questionnaire, and their roles.
- Only collect information you can handle and use.
- Questionnaires can be a useful method of collecting information from a large number of people.
- The response rate to questionnaires can be very low unless people are committed to contributing to the process through understanding its purpose.
- Questionnaires with closed questions or structured to elicit yes/no responses, ticks in boxes, a choice from limited options, or a score on a scale, produce data that can be readily quantified and are fairly easy to manage.
- Questionnaires with open questions asking for views, opinions, suggestions or descriptions generate much more anecdotal information or unique responses that can be difficult to analyse, collate and/or draw conclusions from.
- Consider whether or not the questionnaire can be anonymous. People may feel more able to be open and honest if it is; on the other hand you may need to be able to identify them, their department, the type of job and so on in order to be able to act on any findings.
- Some assurance about the confidentiality of replies to questionnaires and how this will work can help encourage people to reply and to do so openly.
- Not everyone will have the same level of literacy skills, so the language and construction of the questionnaire may need to take this into account.
- The more targeted a questionnaire is (for example, to specific groups of staff, people doing particular jobs, a section of a department), the more specific the questions can be and the more closely particular aspects of a situation can be investigated.
- A questionnaire can be a relatively simple means of collecting information quickly from a large number of people; on the other hand, if it is badly prepared it is likely to be confusing, generate random data that cannot be managed or fail to provide the information it was intended to collect. If in any doubt about developing a questionnaire it is wise to get specialist help.
- If people are being asked to put time and effort into completing a questionnaire they will want to know the outcome as quickly as possible. Schedule the process of collecting, collating, analysing and producing

findings, and agree when, how and to whom the findings will be communicated.

Observation

- Observing people at work and the process and procedures they operate can be an effective way of spotting risks or hazards which people doing the jobs are so familiar with that they may not recognize them.
- Decide what information you want.
- Agree who will undertake the observation, for example, managers, supervisors, a joint management–staff team, consultants.
- A brief needs to be prepared for observers explaining what to look for and how to record findings.
- Recording findings has to be consistent if the information provided is to be comparable from all the observers and manageable.
- People may be inhibited by being observed or may do things in a way they do not normally do them; an observer can influence simply by being there.
- Observation can be time-consuming and/or costly if a reasonable cross-section of people or jobs is to be observed in order to provide reliable data.
- Staff being observed need to be clear about the purpose of the observation: what information will be used, how and by whom, how confidentiality will apply, and so on. Otherwise they may not feel able to cooperate.
- Decide in what form and to whom observers will report their findings at the outset so the task can be appropriately organized.
- Agree how the findings will be communicated generally.
- If outside consultants undertake the observation they can bring a degree of objectivity that people familiar with the organization and its operation may not have.
- Consultants may be more acceptable as observers to staff and management if they are perceived as being independent, having specialist expertise and are working to a jointly agreed brief.
- Deciding (jointly) to use outside observers without the knowledge of staff is also an option. This has certain obvious advantages but raises many issues about openness and involvement.

Structured interviews

- Structured interviews, done well, can provide the best of both worlds: one-to-one interaction with control of the information generated by using agreed questions and recording systems throughout.
- As with all methods it is important to be clear about the information required and in what form it should be collected.

- Structured interview questions can be 'closed', requiring the interviewer to tick choices, circle responses or underline from a list. Questions can also be 'open', where the interviewer's task is more complex. In this case a recording process that picks out key points, facts, feelings, views or other information relative to the question is helpful. Keeping even 'open' questions limited in scope and specific makes recording easier.
- Interviewing people is a good way of getting them to 'open up' about problems, risks they perceive, their fears and concerns, experiences they have had, or obtaining detailed information about practice.
- Interviewing can be very time-consuming if done well.
- Structured interviewing, because it is built around previously agreed questions and recording processes, can become mechanistic if the interviewers are not skilled.
- A carefully designed recording process is as important as carefully designed questions if it is to produce consistent, accurate and manageable data from all the interviews.
- Structured questions and recording processes help to ensure the objectivity of the interviewers.
- Decide who will do the interviewing. The interviewers need to be skilled, or to be trained, and they need to be acceptable to the interviewees as well as people who will use the information and the findings they generate.
- Jointly agreeing and/or developing and designing the structured interviews with employee representatives can help ensure cooperation and the acceptability of the results.
- Employees should be informed about the structured interview process, its purpose and their role in contributing to it.
- Interviewers and interviewees need to be clear about how and to whom information gathered will be passed, and how any agreements on confidentiality will be managed.
- Recording of interviews using cassette tapes is a possibility. However, this may inhibit people and they will still have to be listened to again in order to transfer responses to a recording system for analysis.
- Structured interviews with groups is a means of gathering a range of views at one time, but they are difficult to manage and require a very skilled interviewer and/or very sophisticated recording techniques.
- Time invested in the planning and design of structured interviews is essential if the reward is to be useful and usable information.
- If the expertise to develop a structured interview process is not available in the organization, you should consider obtaining outside help or employing consultants with the appropriate expertise.

Working groups

- Group approaches to identifying possible risks or hazards can work very well because managers, staff representatives, people working in particular areas or jobs, safety officers and so on can all be involved and bring their different perspectives to bear. However, if the group is too big it will be unmanageable.

- A working group will need clear terms of reference, clearly defined tasks, roles and power, resources to do the job, and a timetable.

- The group will need to be clear about what is expected from it as a final product, in what form, for whom and how it will be used, in order to organize their tasks appropriately.

- It is important to be clear from the start what the status of the findings of the group will be.

- As with any working group there is a risk that it may become a 'talking shop' or develop a life of its own! Avoid this by putting time and effort into setting it up properly with finite tasks and an agreed timescale wherever possible.

- Information about the working group should be communicated to employees to ensure they know what is going on and why, how the group will work, and their role in contributing to the work of the group.

- Working groups can employ a range of methods in their investigation; they will need to be clear about how the information generated in different ways will be brought together.

- The variety of members in a working group can be helpful in that different members may be more or less acceptable to different employees because of their skills, experience, being known by the people, or their representative roles. Thus tasks can be allocated to the most appropriate person to get the best possible results.

- A working group that is representative may be more generally acceptable as everyone can feel their views are being fed into the process. In addition, the findings of a representative group may be generally 'owned', or more so than those of differently constituted groups.

- The working group will need to gain the confidence of employees, so they need to be able to explain their role and task, how the outcomes will be used and how issues such as confidentiality will be managed.

- Communicating the findings of the group needs to be planned as part of their task, including communicating generally with employees.

Consultants

- Identifying consultants to undertake an investigation on your behalf can be helpful as you can select people with the particular skills you require, for example, experts in safety matters, specialist researchers.
- Using consultants can be a speedy and cost-effective way of working if properly managed, because they can devote time and attention to the process that few employees have; thus the cost may be less than using employees.
- When choosing a consultant you need to be sure you have the right person or persons for the job:
  - check their track record and experience;
  - make sure the approach they will use is acceptable;
  - ensure they can meet your timescale;
  - check that you can provide the support and resources needed;
  - confirm that it is a cost-effective option;
  - ensure their style is appropriate for your organization.

- You must brief consultants properly and fully: this means you must be clear about what you are trying to achieve. The brief should cover:
  - what you expect them to achieve – be precise about the task, problem, needs, and so on;
  - terms of reference;
  - the outcomes you require and in what form;
  - what you want to do with the outcomes;
  - timescale they are to meet;
  - what you or others will do to support or assist them;
  - who will manage their work, to whom they report, when and how;
  - what resources are available to them;
  - how you expect them to work and with whom;
  - how issues such as confidentiality will be dealt with.

  Clearly a formal contract is preferable when working with consultants, so much of the briefing information can be included in that.
- It is essential to communicate to employees about the consultants, their task and role. Otherwise they may be perceived as 'management spies' and people may not feel they can cooperate fully.
- It may be worthwhile agreeing on the task and the consultant(s) in a joint forum with employees or their representatives. In this way the consultant(s) can work on behalf of the joint group.
- Beware of 'dumping' the responsibility for the investigation on consultants. Consultants should work *with* you if the investigation is to be effective, not take over and do the job for you.

- Remember that the problems and issues identified by the consultants are the responsibility of the organization, and you will need to agree how you will act upon the findings of the consultants.
- You will need to agree a way of communicating the consultants' findings.

References

1   Health and Safety Executive (1988), *Preventing Violence to Staff*, London: HMSO.
2   Rowett, C. (1986), *Violence in Social Work*, Cambridge: Institute of Criminology.
3   Toon (1994), 'GPs demand action on wave of violent attacks', *Pulse*, Vol. 54, No. 14, 9 April.
4   Morgan, M.M. and Steedman, D.J. (1985), 'Violence and the accident and emergency department', *Health Bulletin*, Vol. 43, No. 6, pp. 278–82.

7 Developing a policy

The Health and Safety at Work Act 1974 places certain obligations on employers and employees with respect to safety at work (see Chapter 5). Probably the best way of translating those obligations into responsibilities and actions to be taken is by developing a formal, written policy.

In this sense a policy is a document that sets out the course of action to be pursued by the organization (employers and employees) in order to fulfil its obligations in law and in terms of national or workplace agreements.

A policy provides a framework on which procedures and practices can be built. It makes it possible to require or demand appropriate behaviour or action in relation to safety matters. Furthermore, a policy provides clarity, demonstrates commitment and develops confidence in the organization's willingness to address the issue of violence at work. While the responsibility for policy is a managerial one, the usual, and generally most effective, process for developing policy is a joint one, where management and staff negotiate and agree it.

Developing any policy, especially where meeting its requirements can have a cost to the organization (in financial, resource or time terms), or to the individual (in terms of demands on them, required behaviour, changes in practice), can be fraught with difficulty. The management and staff roles in negotiating it can become adversarial and time-consuming. The consultative process can be extremely protracted. Worst of all, the policy can end up so watered down in becoming acceptable that it does not achieve its purpose. Having said all that, a policy that is not jointly developed, negotiated and agreed is unlikely to be 'owned' by people generally, so it may not have their commitment or confidence.

Before starting the process of developing the policy it is helpful to be clear about who needs to be involved in the development process and how. Thought should be given as to whether those involved should be management, staff representatives, administrative and reception staff, and/or specialist staff. Their powers and remit will need to be agreed and decisions made about who should be party to agreements. This can include managers with delegated authority, trade union representatives, and representatives of non-union staff.

Agreement will need to be reached on the timescale for the development, the consultation process and finalization of the policy. This will depend to a large extent on the resources and support that will be required throughout the process and the limited availability of busy people, which can slow the process considerably. Being clear about the priority given to this task and planning meeting dates will help the group to keep to the timescale. The tasks may not be straightforward or easy, and people who commit themselves to assisting in the process should understand what their commitment entails.

Those involved will need to realize that the agreed policy may mean changes or costs that people will wish to resist. Management and the development group need to be very clear about the extent to which they must take others' views into account and the extent to which they may impose their own.

The policy document

The areas that would normally be covered by a policy on violence at work are identified below.

Policy title

The policy title needs to make it clear what the policy is about in general terms. Examples of titles include: 'Combating Violence at Work'; 'XYZ Trust Policy on Violence to Staff'; 'Safety from Violence at Work – a Policy Statement'; 'Health and Safety Policy – Violence to Staff'.

If the policy on violence to staff is part of an overall health and safety policy it ought to be identifiable within the main policy, and an obvious title can help.

The purpose (or aim or objective)

This should be a general statement of what the policy is intended to achieve. It does not need to go into any detail. For example, the purpose could be described as follows:

- to prevent the risks to staff from violence;
- to fulfil legal and other obligations by ensuring the safety of staff;

- to protect staff from all forms of violence whenever possible and provide after-care should staff be subjected to violence;
- to ensure that everyone in the organization is aware of and fulfils their responsibility for safety from violence at work.

Definition

This should set out what the organization and this particular policy means by violence at work. It should indicate what behaviour and actions are included and excluded from the definition of violence used (see Chapter 4).

The philosophy

This should describe the basis from which the policy starts: the values and beliefs underlying it that can be expressed as a series of statements, for example:

- All violence to staff is unacceptable, whatever form it takes and whatever reasons are cited for it.
- We recognize the risks to staff from violence at work and the obligations of the organization to minimize the risks.
- Dealing with, or being subject to, violent behaviour is not considered to be a failure on the part of an employee.
- Violence is not considered to be an acceptable part of any job, nor is it part of the duties of any employee to accept violent behaviour.
- We recognize the potentially damaging effects of violence on individuals, work performance and the organization as a whole, and are committed to combating it.

Whom the policy covers

All staff in the organization may be subject to the policy and its requirements, or it may be a policy developed for a particular site, department or group of staff with a unique role in the organization.

It is also important to be clear about whether the policy applies to permanent staff only, or also to contracted staff, temporary staff, locums, consultants or others who may be working in the organization for a short time.

What the employer is committed to do

Examples of the actions that the employer will take include:

- Analysis/audit within the organization to identify risks, hazards, problems or other issues.

- Preventive measures to combat the risks of violence at work, such as changes in the environment, procedures and practices.
- Data collection or monitoring of incidents of violence to staff and actions as a result of the information gathered.
- Communication of the policy to ensure that everyone is aware of it and their responsibility in respect of it.
- Allocation of specific roles and responsibilities in support of the policy, such as: assigning a manager with overall responsibility for the policy; responsibility for monitoring incidents; responsibility for ensuring appropriate after-care for staff who experience violence; responsibility for safety training.
- Sanctions to be taken in the event of violent behaviour by an employee of the organization.
- Formal written warning to be given to any individual who has made threats of violence towards an employee; this warning should indicate that legal action may be taken if there is a breach of the law.
- After-care procedures to be made available, such as: counselling; time off work; earnings protection; help in bringing a court case; assistance with compensation claims or medical assistance.
- Evaluation and review of the policy and procedures at agreed intervals, and the continual development of practice.
- Putting in place an appropriate joint management–staff forum with a health and safety remit or a specific remit in relation to violence at work.
- Training of staff to ensure that they can fulfil their responsibilities under the policy and protect themselves from violence at work. This should also cover the issue of restraint in residential and day-care settings.

What is required of individuals

This section could contain a general statement outlining the obligation of employees to take reasonable care of themselves and other people who may be affected by their acts or omissions. Other areas which could be covered include:

- The requirement to operate procedures as specified, such as entry procedures, wearing of badges, notification to reception of visitors expected, booking in and out of the workplace, use of a diary system, and so on.
- Attendance at training events covering: the policy; the implementation of procedures; systems for reporting incidents of violence; more specialist events for managers, front-line staff, travelling staff or other groups.

- Reporting of incidents of violence using the procedures available to them.
- The particular roles of individuals, for example, supervisors, line managers, personnel staff, safety or welfare staff, and training staff.
- Reporting of hazards, risks or problems that individuals identify or become aware of in the course of their work.

Performance measures

The inclusion of performance measures within the policy means that the effectiveness of the policy can be assessed against them. Performance measures include:

- A reduction in the number of incidents, attacks, assaults or injuries over a given period.
- A reduction in the proportion of staff assaulted in a given time or particular area of work.
- A reduction in the number of working days lost as a consequence of incidents of violence.
- Fewer staff feeling concerned or afraid of violence at work, or a raised level of morale (this may require a survey or other analysis before and after the implementation of the policy so that comparisons can be made).
- A reduction in the rate of increase in incidents of violence to staff.
- Fewer staff leaving because of fears of violence or actual violence (exit interviews are one way of gathering this information).
- Reductions in compensation claims or payments or insurance premiums.

Performance measures can be developed for the whole organization, parts of it, or specific types of work. They are particularly useful in assessing the effectiveness of newly developed procedures. Performance measures that can help to demonstrate such effects as fewer working days lost, higher morale, greater productivity or lower turnover of staff assist in justifying the costs of security equipment, providing transport, changing procedures, or other measures taken to combat violence at work.

Evaluation/review

The policy itself should include information about how its effectiveness will be assessed. It could give details of who will take responsibility, when assessment will take place, the process that will be used, and how the results will be communicated to people and acted on.

Similar methods to those used in investigating the risks of violence at work (see Chapter 6) can be used in evaluation, including questionnaires, group meetings, observation and structured interviews.

An evaluation process based directly on assessment against performance measures within the policy can be developed. Evaluation data can also be obtained from data generated by other systems such as personnel systems – for example, staff turnover figures, exit interview reports or evidence of fewer problems in recruiting staff.

In addition, when a violence at work incident-reporting system is in place (see Chapter 9), this will provide direct data on the scale of the problem and any changes in it, including an increase or decrease in people seeking some sort of after-care.

Finally, in developing a new policy it is wise to incorporate the first review date into the policy, to ensure that a review does in fact take place. Thereafter reviews should be at regular intervals but may not need to be very frequent.

Resource implications

It is clear that a properly organized system to ensure the personal safety of employees will involve some costs. Measures for dealing with violent incidents, and for providing after-care and support to those involved, all have resource implications. Employers will need to examine the cost implications of those procedures which can contribute to, or reduce, the risk of violence towards staff.

Although health care takes place round the clock, the number of staff working overtime or beyond normal office hours will need to be reviewed to check whether these patterns of work are really necessary, and steps may be needed to avoid over-reliance on staff working overtime – perhaps by recruiting additional workers or by the redeployment of existing staff. Staffing levels will need reappraisal so that there is the capacity to provide additional support in potentially violent situations, for example by making arrangements for joint home visits.

When deciding on establishment levels generally, account should be taken of holiday and training commitments, as well as cover for staff absences through illness. Arrangements of this kind help to avoid dangerous difficulties and delays in providing temporary cover or support.

The provision of counselling where individuals have experienced violence is also likely to involve reallocation of staff time, and the services of a paid counsellor from within or outside the agency.

Developing an effective personal safety strategy and preparing and supporting staff to play their part will involve awareness-raising and training for staff at all levels. Health care agencies already face heavy demands on their training resources. New legislation, for example the NHS and Community Care Act 1990, and new ways of organizing and delivering health care carry with them a need for extensive staff training.

The introduction of personal safety training, as part of an organization's personal safety strategy, cannot be achieved without the commitment of additional resources. Rather than being seen as yet another area to be added to a long list of training needs, it is helpful to recognize that personal safety underpins good practice with each patient group. Effective use of scarce resources, including professional staff, will be enhanced where the workers are confident and well-supported, and where opportunities for violent behaviour are kept to a minimum.

Health care provider agencies, whether Directly Managed Trusts, NHS Trusts, or private or not-for-profit organizations, all face spending constraints and may not relish yet further demands on scarce resources. Nevertheless, employers have a clear legal and moral duty to secure the safety of their staff and to reduce the chances of compensation claims arising. Additional resources will need to be set aside in order to provide a safe working environment.

8 Implementing a policy

Developing and agreeing a policy is a vital step towards a coherent organizational response to violence at work, but it is only one step. Policies often stop at the point where they are statements of intent and, while the intentions are good, little action follows because of the lack of procedures.

The policy itself says *what* people will do; the procedures then go on to say *how* they will do things. The procedures required will depend on what the policy says, the nature and scale of the problem of violence at work in the organization, and the size, culture and the nature of work of the organization. The procedures that may need to be stipulated include:

- how particular jobs or tasks should be performed, for example:
  - reception duties;
  - interviewing members of the public;
  - storage and dispensing of medicines;

- working practices, such as:
  - notification of and receiving visitors;
  - wearing of identification badges;
  - controlling access to buildings or parts of them;

- working patterns, for example:
  - working within or outside the office, and the use of diary sheets, signing-in and signing-out systems;
  - security procedures when working late;
  - working in other people's homes or premises;
  - travelling on business;

- how to obtain security equipment, including:
    - mobile telephones/car telephones;
    - personal alarms;
    - two-way radios;

- how to deal with tradespeople, contractors and deliveries, such as:
    - nominated contact person in charge of people working on premises;
    - checks or vetting of people who will work in the organization;
    - reception of people into the organization and systems for identifying them while they are working;

- how to provide training in support of the policy, such as:
    - induction;
    - general health and safety;
    - communication skills;
    - interpersonal skills;
    - assertiveness training;
    - how to operate procedures;
    - practical techniques for protection;
    - specialist training, for example, counselling;
    - managers' roles in policy implementation;

- how to monitor incidents of violence, including:
    - a reporting system;
    - a report form;
    - a nominated member of staff responsible for reports and monitoring information;
    - the use of monitoring information;

- how to follow up incidents of violence and provide after-care, for example:
    - actions the organization will take to assist staff who are subjected to violence directly, such as time off work, protected earnings;
    - services the organization will obtain, for example, counselling;
    - support available for staff who have been assaulted or threatened, for example, legal advice, medical assistance;

- routine safety checking, such as:
    - security arrangements for drugs;
    - locking up, nominated keyholders, setting alarms;
    - testing of safety equipment;
    - maintenance and repair of safety equipment or systems;

- reporting faults or risks to people responsible for safety precautions;
- evaluation/review of the policy, including:
  - when such evaluations/reviews will take place;
  - who is responsible for evaluation and review and how it will be undertaken;
  - how the results will be communicated.

The procedures should set out in detail how managers should respond after an act of violence. The immediate priority will be to ensure that another incident does not occur. In a surgery situation, for example, this may involve asking the violent person to leave.

In hospital and other residential settings, immediate exclusion may not be an option. Any action should balance the need to avoid condoning violence with the need to avoid precipitating any further incident. Priority must be given to preventing a recurrence and assisting the injured person.

9 Reporting violent incidents

Effective reporting and monitoring of incidents are identified by Poyner and Warne[1] as the single most important factor in attempting to make workplaces and staff safer.

The problem of under-reporting

The under-reporting of violent incidents is a significant problem in monitoring such attacks and developing responses, and its importance cannot be over-emphasized. Unless there are accurate records, the case for additional resources for developing a safety strategy is difficult to make.

A number of surveys have revealed heavy under-reporting of violent incidents involving medical professionals and their patients. There are a number of reasons why people fail to report violence. In some instances they feel that the incident reflected on their own competence and that reporting it will draw their 'failure' to the attention of others. In a number of studies workers have indicated that they did not report an incident because they saw such happenings as 'normal' in their work setting. Where there is a constantly raised level of violence, staff wonder whether to report every incident, or none at all.

In some areas the local political climate may encourage a culture of problem denial, with staff feeling under pressure not to report incidents which they feel reflect adversely on them or on their employing organization.

Similarly the ethos of an organization may militate against staff reporting violence. Fear of appearing to be unable to cope with aggression can be a major hazard in achieving a true picture of the nature and extent of violence. There is often an unrealistic expectation that men in particular should be able to handle potentially violent situations.

Some staff have said that they had experienced, or feared, unhelpful responses from management, including blaming the victim, failing to recognize the seriousness of the situation, and suggesting that the worker had over-reacted in some way. In Crane's study[2] of those staff who reported violence to managers, only 40 per cent received what they considered to be a satisfactory response, although almost all reported a supportive response from other colleagues.

These findings highlight the need for managers to accept responsibility for preventing and responding to violence in a positive and staff-supportive manner. Safety awareness training, and training on making effective use of agreed procedures and guidelines, should be routine for all managers in health care settings.

Some people find it particularly difficult to report or discuss incidents of sexual abuse or threats. Another factor is the fear of further damaging the relationship between the health care professional and the patient. In some cases the worker fears that reporting the incident will lead to prosecution of the attacker, and is unwilling to set the process in train.

In the 'File on 4' radio programme broadcast in May 1994[3] Carol Kedward of the University of Sussex suggested that under-reporting could be linked with a tendency for victims of violence generally to blame themselves. Examples include victims of domestic violence or of child abuse who often feel that violence has occurred because of something they have done.

People working in the caring professions are notoriously reluctant to ask for help from others; their work is stressful, however, and it is all too easy for staff to tolerate negative or threatening behaviour.

Those working in the medical and related professions have a responsibility to themselves and their colleagues to help prevent violent incidents. Part of this responsibility involves the reporting of any incidents which do occur. People need to be assured that it is not a sign of personal or professional failure to be attacked or threatened, and reminded that under-reporting or secrecy can expose themselves and other staff to serious risk. Information about incidents will also help in the development of effective strategies for preventing violence, and help in the design of personal safety training programmes.

The GMSC[4] (General Medical Services Committee) strongly recommends that all violent incidents are reported to the police. In *Combating Violence in General Practice* the point is made that:

'If doctors fail to take decisive action in the face of actual or threatened violence, they not only do a disservice to themselves, their staff and other colleagues, but they put at risk the mutual trust on which primary care is based.'

The Health and Safety Commission issued a consultative document early in 1994 which included a proposal to make incidents of violence at work reportable under the revised Reporting of Injuries, Diseases and Dangerous Occurrences Regulations (RIDDOR). If the proposal is accepted this could be invaluable in providing relevant and reliable data.

Reporting systems

Reporting systems can aid investigation of risks at work where they are already used, or they may be developed as part of the procedures for implementing policy.

Some organizations use existing accident report systems to record incidents of violence. There are drawbacks to the use of accident report systems for this purpose, however. Accident reports are not generally filed unless actual injury results from the incident, so their use can give a false picture of the level of violent incidents and lead to a false sense of security. The use of accident forms contributes to a perception that only incidents where someone has suffered a serious medical or financial loss should be reported. It often does not register that there is an equal and important need to record threats, racial abuse and other forms of harassment.

A separate system using a form specifically to record violent incidents usually works best. A simple form that can be completed by, or on behalf of, someone subjected to violence provides information that can be analysed and used in the development of future preventive measures. Useful information to collect on the form includes:

- Time, day and date of the incident, as this may help identify peak periods of risk, patterns of incidents at certain times, or people at risk because of the times they work.
- A sketch or description of the location of the incident can sometimes help identify design flaws that can be rectified.
- An account of what happened leading up to and during the incident can, for example, highlight a need for back-up staff or security staff; indicate where normal practice leaves staff vulnerable to attack; suggest that alarms or panic button systems are required, or that training is needed to help staff operate existing procedures or develop skills in managing potentially violent people.
- Asking the individual concerned to describe the attacker can sometimes help identify particular sections of the public who represent a risk to staff.
- Attempting to identify causes and motives may help to suggest where systems and procedures trigger violence, for example:

- when people have been kept waiting;
- where people cannot get access to someone they believe can help;
- when documentation or letters are not understood.

● The name and details of the employee attacked, although it may be decided that forms can be completed anonymously. Employee details should include details of gender and ethnicity. Currently there is little hard evidence of the number of attacks which have a racial content. An analysis of reporting information can provide an indication of whether there are racial issues which need particular attention.

Once a form has been designed it is best to start using it to see how well it works. It may be necessary to redesign the form in the light of early experience of its use.

As the report of the incident is not the end of the matter it is sensible to keep records of the effects of the incident on the worker and property, as well as details of follow-up actions taken and after-care for the staff member. This information can be kept separately or on the reverse of the incident report form and completed by the person responsible, for example the personnel manager, safety officer or nominated manager.

The incident report form must remain confidential; people will not feel inclined to report incidents unless they feel sure that their privacy will be protected. Monitoring information or details for management reports can still be extracted from the incident report forms without identifying the staff concerned.

It is essential that all employees are aware of the procedures for reporting violent incidents. They will need to know who has overall responsibility for the procedure and how to obtain an incident report form. Guidance about how this should be completed should be provided, together with information about where to get help if this is needed, and what should be done with the completed form.

Information should also be provided to all staff about whom they should go to for advice, help and support or for any of the after-care services, and how they will receive information about any follow-up action taken when an incident has been reported.

An example of an incident report form can be found in Appendix B (p. 219).

References

1   Poyner, B. and Warne, C. (1986), *Violence to Staff – A Basis for Assessment and Prevention*, Health and Safety Executive, London: HMSO.
2   Crane, D. (1986), 'Violence on social workers', *Social Work Today*, Social Work

Monographs, Colchester: University of East Anglia.
3   British Broadcasting Corporation, 'File on 4', programme no. 94VY3020NHO, transmitted 17 May 1994.
4   General Medical Services Committee (1994), *Combating Violence in General Practice*, London: BMA.

10 The workplace

This chapter contains a series of guidelines on good practice in relation to personal safety for health care workers in the workplace. Whilst the guidance provided is directed at employers and employees in a variety of health services settings, much is equally relevant in a range of other employment situations.

The environs

Employers and employees sometimes forget that the environs of the workplace – the grounds, gardens and parking areas – are still part of the premises and need to be considered in terms of safety. Even where the surrounding areas are not part of the employer's premises, employee safety in these areas should still be considered; after all, they are only there because this is their place of work.

Visibility is an important issue in grounds and car parks: people need to be able to see and be seen. Proper lighting is an essential part of ensuring visibility, but it will only be of limited use if people are obscured by walls, fencing or vegetation. It may be necessary to consider opening up areas or barriers by removing walls and fences and keeping hedges and bushes pruned. If car parks are multi-storey they need to be well-lit everywhere, particularly in stairways. Where the employer does not own the car park used by employees, then representation should be made to the owners so that it can be made safer.

Some organizations provide preferential parking for women drivers so they can be nearer to the buildings and avoid parking in the potentially more risky areas. Indeed some organizations earmark all their immediate parking for women drivers, while men must park in public car parks when space in the private car park is not available.

In one organization the only access to the private rooftop car park after office hours was via a public multi-storey car park that was dark, dingy and threatening for most people. As staff who during the day travelled by train on business often returned after office hours, the organization agreed to pay for them to park at the station, even though it was very close to the free private car park.

Sometimes protecting the grounds and car parks of a workplace with fencing or walls is feasible and worthwhile. An entry card system can be used, with gates or barriers allowing employees' vehicles to enter or leave, or they can be controlled by security staff.

Video surveillance of grounds and car parks is now more common. It enables security or other designated staff to see what is happening outside from a safe point. Any incident can be reported immediately and/or the security staff can go to the aid of someone in difficulty.

Thought should be given to items left around in car parks or grounds; all sorts of everyday items are potential weapons. Some, such as gardening tools, are very dangerous when misused.

Sensor-activated additional lighting can be useful, as staff can run into brightly-lit areas. It may also signal to security staff or others inside that something is wrong. External alarm points known to staff could be activated if help were needed. Emergency lighting is worth considering in case of power failure.

Access to the workplace

Access to the workplace very often centres on the main door and reception service. Certainly this area is important, but there are relatively few organizations with only one entrance, controlled by a reception service. Most have back doors, fire doors, service bays, car park entrances, and so on. All these are potential access points into the building, and may well be preferred by anyone with criminal activity in mind.

Even where there is general public access to a building it is possible to confine that access to public areas, so that employees come to the public rather than find members of the public wandering around the building. Limiting access can be achieved by using:

- locked doors that can be operated by a key, key card or access number punched in by staff;
- one-way doors; these can be used by staff to exit at any time and to meet fire regulations, but entry can only be effected by use of a key system; if these doors are used as an escape route for staff other doors may also be

needed in case they cannot use the key system in an emergency;
- offices off the reception or waiting area where employees can meet members of the public but can see, and be seen by, reception and/or security staff.

Access to buildings (where there is not general public access) or to parts of buildings can also be controlled if:

- all visitors and other callers are notified to reception or security to ensure they are expected;
- visitors and/or tradespersons use the entrance marked;
- visitors sign in and out so it is known who is in the building and when they leave;
- all legitimate visitors wear a pass or visitor's badge;
- all visitors are met by an employee and remain their responsibility throughout the visit;
- 'no entry' signs are used;
- 'staff only' notices are posted;
- staff wear badges in big organizations so they are clearly identified as staff;
- there is a reception or security area on each floor;
- all tradespeople, contractors and deliveries have a named employee contact who is aware of their business and supervises them while on the premises, and:
  - they have appointments;
  - their identity is verified, perhaps by seeking references;
  - there are practice guidelines for them – where they can go, what they can do, required standards of behaviour and sanctions in the contract;
- there is a procedure for dealing with unexpected callers, for example:
  - they are not admitted unless they have an employee contact who will be responsible for them;
  - a nominated employee (for example, the duty officer) sees all other unexpected callers;
  - security staff/volunteers can be called to ensure people leave if necessary.

Hospitals

Hospitals face particular problems about security, with high levels of theft reported annually. There have also been incidents of attacks on in-patients, and the abduction of babies from hospitals.

Many hospitals have multiple points of entry and operate an open access policy for patients and their families and friends. Incidents have occurred in which both hospital patients and staff have been attacked by intruders. A managed access policy will work towards maintaining a balance between keeping access as open as possible to patient care areas, whilst taking steps to reduce the opportunities for intrusion.

The National Association of Health Authorities and Trusts (NAHAT) NHS Security Manual[1] suggests that the following steps may be helpful:

'• where possible, and always with regard to fire escape requirements, patient care areas should be securely locked at night;
• provide reception points on wards, floors and clinic/surgery entrances;
• train staff to challenge all strangers;
• impose a 9.00 p.m. curfew on general visiting in hospital/residential buildings.'

Dealing with access points other than main doors can be difficult. It is often hard to persuade staff to keep back doors and side entrances locked. It is not unusual to find one-way fire doors propped open for the convenience of staff or for ventilation. Apart from breaking fire regulations this leaves the building vulnerable. Delivery or loading bays, vehicle entrances, service entrances and car park doors are also potential access points that people rarely consider from the point of view of staff safety.

Employers should insist that fire doors are kept shut at all times; they should not be used as normal exits unless this is unavoidable. All other side doors, rear doors, doors to car parks or garages can be self-closing/self-locking doors or they can be self-closing one-way doors, like fire doors. Staff may need to be provided with keys or key cards or they may have to learn an entry code if such a system is used.

Delivery or loading bays, vehicle entrances and service entrances are sometimes more difficult to deal with directly. What has proved successful for some organizations is to isolate these work areas from the rest of the workplace. Thus, rather than controlling access *to* them, access *from* them into other areas of the workplace is controlled by the use of locked doors. Access to these areas can also be controlled by using fences or otherwise enclosing them, if it is possible to do so.

Whilst it is important to control access to health care premises, health services are provided in buildings which are usually open to the public. Premises should therefore have entrances clearly signposted, with signs in appropriate languages. They should be well-lit, and none of the measures outlined should compromise wheelchair access.

Reception areas/waiting rooms

Reception areas and waiting areas are very often the public face of an organization for most outsiders, and the majority of people will start their contact with the organization here. If someone has come to sort out a disagreement, deal with a problem, make a complaint, or is there other than by choice, the effect could be quite significant. The way in which people are received when they arrive is likely to increase or reduce feelings of anger or distress.

Evidence from research shows that colour can affect mood and perception. Dark, dingy places feel different from bright, welcoming, warm ones. Institutional colours, such as greys and greens, can lead to certain perceptions of places, or confirm our preconceived ideas of what places (and possibly the people in them, too) are like. Being left to wait in a dark, dingy, cold or grubby room is unlikely to improve anyone's mood. A bright, warm, comfortable setting will not guarantee good humour, but it is likely to be calming rather than irritating.

Just as the environment can affect people coming into it as visitors, it can also affect people who work there, even to the point of predisposing them to behaviour that may elicit an aggressive response. A number of organizations have taken this research seriously and applied it to reception and waiting areas in the following ways:

- using pastel colours;
- putting flowers or plants in waiting areas;
- using light and airy rooms for waiting;
- providing comfortable seating;
- making reading material available;
- providing play areas and good-quality toys for children; provision of black dolls as well as white ones will help in making black families feel welcome;
- playing background music or providing TV;
- installing drinks machines or otherwise making refreshments available;
- ensuring there are toilet and baby-changing facilities;
- installing a telephone so people waiting feel they can still communicate with the outside world;
- avoiding stressful noise, such as loud music, irritating public address systems or machine noise;
- making sure there is adequate and accessible parking so people do not arrive frustrated;
- providing directions, maps, details of money required in car parks, and so on, so people can come prepared.

Organizations that take these sorts of steps believe they are cost-effective and make a difference because:

- difficulty in finding the place, parking, and so on is minimized, and so is frustration;
- people feel welcome and expected;
- it appears that the organization has respect for visitors and concern for their comfort;
- people are less likely to feel anonymous, like a number waiting in line;
- waiting is relatively pleasurable, so people do not become increasingly uncomfortable, tense and irritated;
- providing books, reading material, refreshments, and so on creates diversion and interest and avoids boredom.

Aids to effective communication are of special importance in health care settings. People with sensory disability have reported major problems, particularly with regard to confidentiality where relatives are used to facilitate communication with medical personnel.[2] Attention should be given to the provision of loop systems to assist people with hearing impairment, and lighting should be of a quality to facilitate lip-reading and to assist people with impaired sight. Access to British Sign Language or Makaton and minority language interpreters should also be available, and staff should be aware of how to make arrangements for these.

Many people report that the thing most guaranteed to make them angry and frustrated while waiting is not knowing what is going on or how long they will be expected to wait. Some organizations use a ticket system and a display that shows the progress through the queue of people waiting. People may not entirely like the number approach, but it does help to indicate how close they are to being seen.

Other organizations train receptionists to give callers an estimated waiting time. However, this can backfire if the time is then not adhered to. Another approach is for reception staff to go into waiting areas from time to time with a list of the people waiting and give them a 'status report': for example, 'There are three people to be seen before you'; 'Dr X has one person with her, then she'll see you.' Again this can backfire if one person takes much longer than was expected, but at least people are being given some information, and receptionists can update it from time to time.

Perhaps the most straightforward way of managing waiting time is to arrange appointments whenever possible. It is essential to allow a realistic time for each appointment if such a system is to work; otherwise a queue will build up and people may be even more annoyed because they were on time for their appointments.

Reception staff themselves can be in very vulnerable positions, especially where public access means anyone can walk into the building. Some examples of good practice in reception areas include:

- using wider counters so staff cannot be reached across them;
- raising the height of the floor on the staff side of counters, again to protect them from people reaching over;
- providing a panic button or other alarm system;
- providing security cameras so reception staff can see all areas from a safe position;
- reorganizing office layout so reception staff are visible to other staff;
- making sure reception staff have an escape route should they need it;
- providing entry 'phone/entry camera systems in organizations with limited access;
- locking access to counter-protected reception areas;
- installing one-way doors to reception areas;
- ensuring that receptionists are notified by other employees of all expected visitors; other callers, such as deliveries, tradespeople or contractors, can use a visitor form;
- installing intercom links with back-up from nominated staff – or people can listen in if they see worrying behaviour;
- ensuring that under no circumstances is a receptionist, or any other member of staff, left alone in a building which is open to the public.

Many of these safety and security devices have proven necessary and successful. However, it ought to be remembered that what is meant as protection for staff can seem like a barrier to the patient.

Counters, screens and other devices can trigger aggression or violence in some people when they are perceived as a barrier or block. A balance needs to be achieved between creating a welcoming, calming, unthreatening environment for patients while ensuring the safety of staff. Where that balance lies in any given organization will need to be worked out.

Protective screens

Very careful thought is needed before the introduction of protective screens. Poyner and Warne[3] report that in 1984 Glasgow District Council concluded that 'screens represent an unnecessary barrier between tenants and housing staff and that this barrier causes frustration and resentment among many tenants'.

A decision was made to remove screens gradually from all 15 district offices, retaining them only in areas where cash was handled. This decision was backed up by a package of measures which included:

- careful negotiation with staff representatives;
- attention to the interview environment;
- review of staffing and grades to improve the reception process and cut waiting times;
- training;
- supervision and support.

Implementation of this package of measures resulted in a marked drop in staff concern about violence. This example illustrates the importance of avoiding isolated safety measures, and taking a comprehensive approach to the development of safe working places and practices.

Staff safety issues should be an integral part of decision-making about the external design and location of buildings, as well as their internal design and management.

Interviewing in the workplace

Interviewing, or holding similar meetings with people, is a task that many employees in all sorts of organizations perform in the course of their work. There have been unfortunate incidents of aggressive and violent behaviour in interviews in many different work settings. Good interviewing practice guidelines are derived from a wide range of experience in different work situations including social services departments, estate agent offices, social security offices and police stations. These guidelines are directed at both health care employers and their employees:

- Make sure the interview or consultation is not conducted in isolation, that is, make sure someone knows where you are.
  - use a room in which you are visible to others, for example with glass panels (safety glass in the walls is essential) but where the interviewee cannot be overheard.
- It may not be possible to telephone for help and an alarm or panic button should be installed.
- Make sure the room is well-lit but not over-lit; emergency lights may be needed too.

- Stay near the door – if possible, the room should have two doors.
- All sorts of everyday equipment can provide potential weapons, so keep equipment to the absolute essentials.
- Ensure furniture is comfortable, but robust enough not to be thrown.
- Keep rooms locked when not in use.
- Make sure someone knows exactly who you are seeing – and make sure the patient knows that their presence is a matter of record.
- At the first sign you are in difficulty (because people can see or hear you or you raise the alarm) staff should know who will respond and how, and take immediate action.
- Do not arrange to meet anyone when you will be alone in the building.
- Prevent waiting time before an interview/consultation where possible. If there *is* waiting time, make sure the patient knows when they are likely to be seen and keep them informed.
- At least one interview/consultation room should have facilities to aid hearing-impaired clients, to reduce communication difficulties and consequent frustration.

More detailed guidance on interviewing techniques is given in Part 2 of this book.

Handling medicines

It is sensible for all medicines to be kept in a locked cupboard as they are likely to attract criminal interest. The National Association of Health Authorities and Trusts (NAHAT) Security Manual suggests that developing arrangements for safe and secure medicine storage, particular attention should be paid to:

- keeping the pharmacy as the only procurement point for medicines in hospitals and community clinics;
- methods of ordering medicines;
- the means of delivery, including postal services;
- receipts procedure, including full records;
- storage, whether in bulk in the pharmacy or in smaller quantities elsewhere;
- methods of distribution both within and between hospitals;
- the dispensing and issue of medicines;
- the administration of medicines to patients;
- the disposal of medicines no longer required for whatever reason.'

Handling money or valuables

Staff are sometimes responsible for handling cash, particularly in hospital-based catering areas. If this becomes generally known, there is the risk of assault on employees by people who are not patients. It is important to reduce the handling of cash as far as possible in order to reduce the risk of theft and violence.

In those circumstances where cash is collected, it should be banked regularly, making it far less worthwhile for a thief to attempt theft. Staff should know exactly what to do if there is violence in relation to money. Guidelines should be provided, making it quite clear that the first priority is the safety of staff, rather than the safeguarding of money or other valuables. Alarm systems may also be used so that help can be summoned without the attacker being aware of this.

Storing money or valuables

Where money or valuables are stored as part of the business – for example, in banks or building societies – there are usually very sophisticated forms of security. In premises where money or valuables are only held irregularly, at certain times or for certain purposes, the security is often less well organized. Most offices have a petty cash system which involves the storage of cash for day-to-day expenses and emergency payments, and access and control may be handled in a somewhat casual manner.

Where money is stored in the workplace it is worth considering whether this is strictly necessary. If cash storage can be avoided, it should be. This may involve very regular visits to the bank. Use the following guidance to avoid the risk of theft and violence:

- Money collected should be taken to the bank each day rather than stored on the premises.
- Use should be made of a safe and whatever security measures the circumstances demand, such as alarms, cameras, screens.
- The fact that the premises are protected by security measures should be obvious to any potential attacker.
- Employers should make sure, through providing guidelines, that employees know what to do to protect themselves if the need arises.
- Restrict and control access to the premises, or that part of it where money or valuables are kept.
- Avoid developing a pattern of storing money, for example, when wages are to be paid.

- Where money or other valuables are regularly stored, it is worthwhile seeking specialist security advice. This needs to deal with both the practical security measures and the safety of employees.

Moving money

If moving money or valuables from the workplace is a regular occurrence, it is worth employing a specialist security firm to do so. Although there is clearly a cost involved, the serious injury, or even death, of an employee could be at stake.

Where employees do move money themselves, perhaps from hospital to bank, specialist advice can be obtained from security firms or the police on the particular situation and the risks inherent in it. When using employees to move money, employers should provide guidelines for staff so that they know what to do to protect themselves, making sure they are quite clear that that is their first duty, not to protect the money. Staff carrying money should not do so alone.

It is important to avoid establishing a pattern for the movement of money. The days and time should vary, as should the route and means of transport wherever possible. If a number of different people are used for this task, this can avoid any one specific individual becoming a target for attack.

Some simple practical steps will also help to reduce the likelihood of attack and robbery. For example:

- Provide people with a means of contact such as a mobile telephone or two-way radio. This ensures they can keep in touch, raise an alarm or summon help.
- Let the bank or other premises to which they are going know they are on the way and when to expect them – they can then raise the alarm if necessary.
- Use a call-back system so that the workplace is notified on their safe arrival.
- Think about how money or valuables can best be carried. If a briefcase or bag is carried it can be snatched; however, if it is attached to an employee it may be safe from a snatch thief but could result in the employee being injured by someone attempting to take it.
- Ensure that as few people as possible know when, how and by whom money is moved.
- Ensure that people are clear about how to proceed in the event of an approach or attack; guidelines should stress that staff should protect themselves rather than the money they are carrying.

- Providing personal alarms can also be helpful, provided that they are actually carried and people know how to use them.

Patterns of work

In many health care settings, working late or during the early morning are part of the normal working pattern; in other situations such arrangements occur on a less regular basis. Whatever patterns apply, good practice takes account of the following:

- the provision of transport for employees, especially women, when they are required to work unsocial hours and travel in darkness, when it is very quiet and when there is little public transport;
- the provision of nearby, well-lit and/or controlled car parking;
- well-lit paths to nurses' homes, which should *not* be signposted;
- the use of security staff, particularly when premises are isolated, few people are actually working, at night, in areas of high risk, or where services are prone to attack;
- alarm systems that can be activated in parts of the premises not in use while other parts are in use;
- panic buttons or alarms that can be activated in parts of premises in use even when the main alarm system is unarmed;
- ensuring that people work in pairs at least, and they know who else is/should be on the premises;
- ensuring that people are aware of any callers, contractors, deliveries, and so on, that are expected.

References

1   National Association of Health Authorities and Trusts (1992), *NHS Security Manual*, Birmingham: NAHAT.
2   *A Review of the Need for Interpreting and Other Forms of Communication for Deaf and Hard of Hearing People in Buckinghamshire* (1991), Birmingham: RNID in conjunction with PB Services.
3   Poyner, B. and Warne, C. (1986), *Violence to Staff – A Basis for Assessment and Prevention*, Health and Safety Executive, London: HMSO.

11 Nursing homes and day care settings

The focus of this chapter is on residential work, in nursing homes: but much of its content is also applicable to hospitals and to day care settings. The accumulating evidence of violent incidents in residential and day care settings suggests that special consideration will be needed of the circumstances in which acts of violence arise, and the ways in which to manage the establishment to reduce aggression and deal quickly and effectively with violence when it does occur.

It is worth considering some of the issues which affect nursing home and day care staff. Perhaps the most obvious point is that these settings involve high levels of contact between staff and patients. There are thus much greater opportunities for tensions to develop, and fewer natural breaks to allow for 'cooling down'.

In nursing homes, patients may be under particular stress because of:

- the initial impact of admission, with attendant anxiety and insecurity;
- personal stress resulting from illness;
- pressure of communal living and lack of privacy;
- concerns about continuing contact with family or friends;
- pressure from the peer group;
- testing out of staff and organizational boundaries.

A number of incidents have been recorded where staff have been injured as a result of violence not directed at them, when intervening between two or more residents.

Patients and residents

Violence by elderly, confused patients and residents is an area often under-acknowledged by both staff and employers. This can take the form of sexual or racial abuse, threats, spitting, kicking, biting and hitting.

Staffing

It is an unfortunate fact that many of the most vulnerable people in society are cared for in residential settings by inexperienced or untrained staff. Personal safety strategies will need to address issues of staff recruitment, supervision, support and training.

Inappropriate staff behaviour can include rough handling, confrontational styles of work, and inconsistency in imposition of controls or rules. This sort of behaviour can be exacerbated by low staffing levels resulting in stress, inexperience or lack of staff support.

In some circumstances staff may need to hold patients for the patient's own protection or for the protection of others. It is important to keep a balance between the protection of staff and patients, and the provision of an atmosphere in which patients or residents are stimulated and encouraged to develop and maintain independence.

Restraint can provoke anger and should only be used when there is an immediate and serious danger. Employers and employees should refer to guidelines appropriate to the setting in which they work (see 'Select bibliography' at end of book). Staff will need written agency guidance, backed up by appropriate training, on handling those situations in which restraint may be needed.

Location and design

The atmosphere of a nursing home will depend on a combination of factors – staff, residents and physical conditions. The location and design will have an impact on residents, staff and visitors.

Nursing homes are found in a variety of locations ranging from the isolated, rural 'stately home' to the purpose-built home in a town or city. When planning new services, the question of location should be given very careful thought. Access to shops and leisure facilities will reduce a sense of isolation, and easy access to public transport will help to facilitate contact with relatives and friends.

The design of the building itself can have an enormous influence on the morale of the people who live and work there. The Wagner Report on residential care[1] stressed the need to offer residents privacy, for example by not requiring them to share a bedroom. The key is to design for privacy, but also for companionship. Private bedrooms, rooms in which to entertain visitors, and communal recreational facilities, all contribute to a sense of individual well-being, and healthy group functioning.

Care taken with decorating and furnishing adds to the welcoming atmosphere. Where possible, individual choice about private bedroom colour schemes, and flexibility about having personal possessions, help to personalize the individual's surroundings.

In day care settings, accommodation should be provided for group activities, and also space for individual work or to give 'withdrawal space', to allow tempers to cool.

Management issues

Managers of nursing homes carry responsibility for the performance of staff and for their support and supervision. They should ensure that patients and staff have access to external specialist help and advice, for example from psychologists, psychiatrists and counsellors.

Each establishment should have a clear statement of purpose, and objectives which are publicized and which can be used as a reference point for developing services and supporting staff.

Working patterns will need to reflect the nature of the establishment, as well as the need to protect staff. Staff roles and numbers may need some adjustment, and shift systems will also require attention. Every effort should be made to ensure that rotas do not include split shifts or combinations of nights and long weekends, which make people less able to respond effectively in a crisis.

Arrangements for the reception of visitors should be reviewed. A system will be needed to ensure that visitors are quickly received by a member of staff.

Reference

1   Wagner, G. (1987), *Residential Care – A Positive Choice* (The Wagner Report), London: HMSO.

12 Away from the workplace

Home visits

One of the causes of aggressive and violent behaviour is when people feel that there is an intrusion into their private life. Many health care professionals routinely visit their clients at home, particularly where the patient is elderly, infirm or housebound.

The likelihood of violence against health care workers in other people's homes may depend on why they are there. A health visitor providing active support and assistance to the parent of a child assessed as having special needs is likely to receive a very different reception from a social worker taking a child into care.

In some instances, violence is experienced not at the hands of the patient, but of their relatives. The 1992 *Doctor* magazine survey[1] found that 73 per cent of attacks on GPs during home visits were thought to come from patients or their families.

Whatever the reason for being in someone else's home the cardinal rule is to remember that it is *their* home, *their* territory which is being entered. Under 'normal' circumstances people are in control of their homes and what happens there; the presence of a health worker may change that. People may feel that the worker is invading their space, taking away their power, imposing rules and regulations on them or, quite literally, taking over.

Some general points to bear in mind when planning home visits are:

- Do you *have* to go to the patient's home? Could an arrangement be made whereby transport is provided to bring that person to you? This may be particularly worth consideration if there is a history of poor relationships with the person, or aggressive and violent behaviour, or if the purpose of the visit is likely to cause problems.

- Do you have to go *alone* to someone's home? You could consider taking a colleague with you, although this may be difficult when resources are scarce and workloads heavy.
- Before you visit someone at home, check whether that person has a record of violence. If there is no record, ask other colleagues who have had dealings with the person concerned.
- Before leaving your workplace, make sure people know where you are going, what your plans are, and when you expect to finish a visit and/or return to the workplace. Also, arrange to check in with someone at the workplace. Make sure you take with you notes of telephone numbers, and money or a card for the 'phone if you do not have access to a mobile 'phone.
- Employers could consider providing mobile 'phones or two-way radios for use by staff on such occasions.
- Go in daylight wherever possible.
- When you arrive at the home, think about its location. Is it at the top of a tower block, down a country lane, in a one-way street? Consider where you should park your car so you can leave quickly, or the nearest route to public transport or a busy, well-lit place.
- At the person's home remember you are the visitor; say who you are, where you are from and show some identification if you have it. Don't make assumptions; follow these guidelines:

    - Check who you are talking to.
    - Make sure you are expected, or at least that it is understood why you are there.
    - Don't march in; wait to be asked or ask if you can go in.
    - Whenever possible acknowledge it is the other person's home and territory: let them lead the way, take your coat, invite you to sit down, introduce other people.
    - If you get an aggressive reception at the door, or the patient appears to be drunk or otherwise out of control, you could decide not to enter the house, or leave immediately without conducting your business.
    - Take only what is essential into a house; leave handbags, medical bags, briefcases and so on elsewhere if this is possible. Also, avoid taking anything that you would not wish a householder to see or read.
    - In the house, take in your surroundings; if at all possible place yourself with a clear line to an exit.
    - Try to avoid reacting to the house itself – for example, if it smells, is very untidy or dirty.
    - At all times remain alert to changes in moods, movements and expressions.

- Do not spread your belongings about; if you need to leave quickly you may not have a chance to collect them.
- If you feel at risk, leave as quickly as possible. If you are prevented from leaving you may wish to try to control the situation, or you may have to fight back (see Chapter 16, 'Coping with violence').
- Do what is necessary to protect yourself – you must not worry about failure.

Any concern about violence from a patient should be discussed with colleagues/manager, to consider what steps should be taken to provide a service whilst safeguarding staff. These may include allocation of the patient to someone already known to and accepted by them.

Other people's premises

Going to conduct business on other people's premises has some parallels with visits to other people's homes. The worker is on someone else's territory, and may be more or less welcome depending on the nature of the visit. Health professionals may have calls to make at local employers' premises, police stations, courts, prisons, hospitals, social services premises, schools, voluntary organizations' offices, hostels, nursing homes and day care centres. Many of the points made in the previous section apply to visiting or working in others' premises. The following additional points should be borne in mind:

- If a stranger rings to arrange a meeting it should be routine procedure to call back to check the details of the name, agency, address, telephone number, and so on.
- If you have any doubts or concerns on arrival at any meeting, telephone your workplace and leave details of where you are and how you can be contacted. Make it obvious that your whereabouts and schedule are known.
- You could have a previously agreed 'distress' signal so that you can summon help without compromising your safety.
- Only go to other organizations' premises in normal working hours when the premises are in use.
- When you are on the premises, try to ensure you know where you are and how to get out.
- If you are in a quiet or isolated part of the premises, stay within easy reach of an exit; preferably sit close to a door.
- Make sure you know in advance the means of transport you will use to get back to your workplace.

- If you are in any doubt, leave the premises if you can; if you cannot get out make as big a fuss as is necessary to attract attention and get help.
- If you have previously had concerns or problems, or been harassed in any way when visiting or working in particular premises, do not hide it because you feel a failure or that you are over-reacting. Tell colleagues or superiors, and arrange for someone else to go with you or in your place next time.
- Avoid going out for meals or to other sites with anyone you are not absolutely sure about. If you must go, make sure you let your work-place know your plans and that the person(s) you are with are aware that you have done this.

Working from home or at home

It is increasingly common for workers, including health professionals, to undertake some work at home. A busy individual may, for example, arrange to complete a detailed report at home, or catch up on essential reading away from the interruptions of the office. For tasks such as these, work at home is often an efficient use of time.

The following guidance is for the individual worker when working at home:

- Use only initials and surname on your doorbell and in the 'phone book. You may even decide you do not want your name on the bell and remain ex-directory so you do not appear in the 'phone book; Directory Enquiries will not give out your number.
- A Yale-type lock can be easily opened; fit a deadlock conforming to British Standard 3621. Make sure the door and frame are strong enough to withstand an attack at the locking points.
- Never leave keys in 'safe' places under plant pots, on ledges or under doormats.
- Never give keys to people working in or delivering to your home.
- Fit a spyhole to the door.
- Ensure any callers you do not know identify themselves, and do check their identity. If you are in any doubt do not let them in.
- Fit a door chain and use it.
- All windows should have locks and be secured when you are out. Secure them also when you are in, unless you need them open and can keep an eye on them.
- Draw curtains and blinds after dark; do not advertise the fact that you are alone.
- If anyone comes to the door for help, such as to use the 'phone, do not

let them in; offer to make the call yourself.

- If you have an alarm system, have panic buttons fitted by the front door, back door, bed or wherever else you think necessary. They will operate the alarm even if it is not armed.
- If you hear strange noises outside your home, do not investigate them yourself, especially after dark; call the police.
- If you lose your keys, change the locks.
- If you go away, cancel papers and milk, arrange to have mail collected, ask a friend or neighbour to call in, and tell the local Neighbourhood Watch or police.

For those who regularly work from home, some additional points to consider are listed below:

- Install a second 'phone line specifically for work so that you can keep your private number confidential; you can switch off the work line or attach it to an answering machine after work hours.
- Use a Post Office box number for all work-related mail so that you do not have to give out your home address.
- Only ever ask people to meet you at your home if you are completely sure you are safe.
- Meet people in public places, their offices or workplaces, but make sure someone knows where you are, with whom, for how long, and when you are expected back. Make sure the person you are meeting is aware that your whereabouts and movements are known.
- Arrange for a friend or neighbour to be a contact whom you can 'phone during the day and report where you are, or, in case of need, who can call where you are expected to be to check you are safe. If you change your plans let your contact know.
- Avoid after-hours meetings.
- Always keep a work diary at home. If you were missing, it could help to trace you, your contacts and your movements.
- Do not go to places or areas where you feel unsafe; always opt for public places, well-lit with lots of people around, rather than quiet backwaters or inner-city areas with high crime rates.
- If you must go to places you feel uneasy about, or to meetings after hours, take someone with you.

Travelling

Health care workers do not work solely in the workplace; many travel to patients' homes, schools, hospitals, hostels, other care agencies, police stations, prisons and the courts. Even where little travel is undertaken, getting to work requires travel on foot, public transport or in a private car. There are inevitable risks involved in travelling.

Employers need to remember that employees travelling on business are still their responsibility, and should consider developing written guidelines and procedures for staff. Safety guidelines about travel are given in Chapter 18.

It is sometimes difficult for employers to implement recording processes so that it is known where staff are, with whom, when they are expected back, and so on, because community health professionals, for example, are accustomed to planning and managing their own time, and may not like having to account for their movements. They may feel they are not trusted and are being checked up on. It is also difficult to remember to amend records and diaries when arrangements are altered, and of course, out-of-date or inaccurate records are worse than no records at all.

Where a procedure is implemented for recording staff visits, it will need to be monitored, and it may be necessary to have sanctions available if it is not followed.

Given these factors, the need to know where people are may have to be 'sold' to employees. They will need to be shown the risks of working alone, being isolated, not being contactable and not being missed. Selling the idea could include providing evidence of what has actually happened to people, using examples from their own workplace of situations where people have been 'missing' or out of touch. It is far better to persuade employees that such recording is needed but, if all else fails, an employer may have to insist it is done.

How the recording is implemented will depend on the particular workplace and work patterns. Before establishing a system the ground rules should be made quite clear, for example:

- No one must ever visit any client or contact without checking they are genuine.
- No one should give out private telephone numbers.
- Everyone must complete a recording form, regardless of the length or type of visit, or whether it involved another person.

Some examples of recording systems that work for organizations are given below:

- A book is kept at the reception desk of the office building and everyone signs in and out. When they sign out they note where they are going, with whom, or whom they are meeting, when they are expected back, and how they can be contacted (for example, a telephone number). The receptionist is responsible for raising the alarm if the person does not return within an hour of the time they were expected, and the person's manager is then responsible for attempting to make contact.

- Every member of staff has a desk diary provided by the organization and is required to fill it in with all details of visits, meetings and so on outside the office. Individuals are responsible for keeping the diary correct, telephoning in changes to secretaries or administrative staff if necessary.
- Each team of staff has a team administrator who is assigned the responsibility for providing a weekly diary sheet which he/she retains. Staff are responsible for notifying the administrator of any changes or any delays in returning. If staff do not return when expected, the administrator notifies the team leader, who then attempts to make contact.

A general warning about revealing personal telephone numbers should be given to all travelling staff or those who work away from their base. If it really is necessary for the employee to be contactable outside working hours, the provision of a mobile 'phone, a pager or a special work 'phone line should be considered.

Detailed travel guidelines for individual workers appear in Chapter 18.

Reference

1   *Doctor* magazine (1992), Vol. 12, No. 19, 5 November.

13 After-care – help and support

The most sophisticated policies and procedures for safety adopted by organizations cannot guarantee that a violent incident will never occur. Since it is impossible to guarantee safety, the development of after-care services that will be available to anyone who is subjected to violence is a sensible step. Such services ensure the organization is able to respond in terms of providing support, practical help and access to sources of specialist help if required. Some of the after-care services that could be developed are outlined below.

Immediately after an incident of violence the person who has been attacked should be asked what he/she needs. Wherever possible, managers and colleagues should ensure that these needs are met. The individual concerned may well, for example, feel the need to leave the workplace at once, and this will involve the provision of alternative staff cover. Where there has been a physical assault the individual concerned should be offered a medical examination as soon as possible.

Debriefing

Research shows that people who have experienced violence need to talk through their experience as soon as possible after the event if long-term trauma is to be avoided. The initial step is to identify people in the organization who will undertake the debriefing (for example, personnel staff, welfare staff, line managers) and train them. Everyone in the organization then needs to know who has been trained for this task and how to contact them. They must be contactable quickly and able to give immediate priority to requests for debriefing at any time.

Important points for a debriefer to remember are:

- Verbal abuse can be just as upsetting as a physical attack.
- Any criticism of the employee's actions with the benefit of hindsight should be avoided.
- What might have been or should have been done in this incident is less important than what can be learnt for the future to avoid a recurrence.
- A debriefer's role is to listen, support and encourage the person who has been subjected to violence to talk; do not expect to 'solve' anything at this stage.
- Debriefers need to know their limits, and when and how it is more appropriate to ask for specialist help.
- Debriefers are not meant to be expert counsellors or psychologists; they are the immediate, first-line help in a process that may go on for some time in some cases.

The knowledge that the organization takes incidents of violence seriously enough to assign and train people as debriefers can encourage employees to report incidents and get the help they need quickly. Debriefing may be a suitable way of providing immediate help for some staff, while others may need specialist help from the outset. The after-care arrangements need to recognize this and not assume that debriefing alone will be adequate in all cases.

Discussion of stressful and painful incidents can help those involved in coming to terms with what has happened, particularly where this is with someone who has had a similar experience. It may be helpful to arrange for the individual who has been subjected to violence to have access to others who have experienced being attacked and who have adjusted and recovered.

People who have been attacked describe a need to talk through the attack, particularly with colleagues who were involved or who witnessed it. Discussing helps to 'make sense' of what happened and to accept its reality. It also acknowledges that violence is an issue for *all* the team.

Departmental and employer responses play a significant part in helping people to recover and resume their professional role. There is a need for evidence that the department takes the incident seriously, and is concerned for the individual worker, as well as for the rest of the team. Letters, cards and flowers are tangible demonstrations of helpful concern and care for the attacked worker.

Counselling

Staff who have experienced violence may need specialist help, or help over a much longer period, that cannot be provided by people within the organization. Some organizations do have internal counselling services for staff.

Others have identified counselling services locally that they can call on when required.

The need for a nominated counsellor to work with staff who have experienced violence is easily overlooked. In most instances it will be appropriate for assistance to be arranged from outside the individual's line management or by employing a professional counsellor on a sessional basis. It can be difficult for feelings of guilt, failure and anxiety about job competence to be discussed with someone from the same agency.

Providing professional counselling is sometimes an essential part of helping people to go through the process of acknowledging what has happened to them, adapting to it and being able to move on. Counsellors can be identified in a number of ways, such as through general practitioners, victim support schemes, local hospitals and the British Association of Counselling. Counsellors should have had specialist training for working with people experiencing post-traumatic stress disorder.

Some organizations have set up reciprocal counselling arrangements with similar agencies which operate, for example, in an adjoining area, so that employees of each agency can receive confidential counselling outside their normal line management structure. Others have agreed that the employee may make his or her own arrangements for professional counselling, with invoices being sent to the employer for payment.

While it will take time and money to provide counselling services, this is a small investment if it avoids future problems for the individual and enables him/her to return to work and to be effective.

Visiting staff who have experienced violence

When staff are off work recovering it is important to keep in touch with them, because they may need debriefing or need other help that the organization can identify and/or supply. They are likely to want to be in touch with work and to know what has happened as a result of the incident, as well as to be reassured that people care about them and do not blame them in any way for what has happened.

When considering visiting it is well worth finding out whom the individual would like to see and when they would like to see them. Some people may need a few days to come to terms with what has happened to them, or reflect on the incident before seeing people from the workplace.

Time off work

Employees who are physically injured as a result of violence obviously need time off work to recover. Some people who suffer no physical injury need time off work too: they may need to come to terms with what happened, recover from shock, or regain their confidence; other people may prefer to go straight back to work.

Employers need to consider how time off work following incidents of violence will be managed. They may decide to set an allowance to apply in all cases, to develop a 'sliding scale' of time off allowed in different circumstances, or to take each individual case on its merits. Dealing with each case individually recognizes that everyone is different, will react differently and will need differing amounts of time to recover. It also allows for periods of regression during the recovery phase.

Although this approach can be more difficult to manage than a policy that gives everyone a set number of days, it will enable those attacked to feel comfortable about recovering at their own pace or taking sufficient time to recover fully. It may also avoid staff suffering any physical or psychological problems in the future as a result of returning to work too quickly.

A phased return to work can help, with clear management agreement about hours worked and specific duties. The possibility of transfer to another location should also be considered if the worker feels anxious about continuing to work in the location of the attack. It is important to recognize that certain situations, such as court appearances, can trigger renewed feelings of stress, and to respond in a helpful and supportive manner.

Managers and colleagues will also need to consider how to deal with continuing contact, and how a service can be provided, where a patient has attacked a health worker.

So far as GPs are concerned, as from 1 April 1994 new rules allow a GP to remove a violent patient from his or her list immediately. Previously there was a seven-day period before such action could be taken. Whilst the new arrangements provide immediate relief for the GP concerned, there remains the issue of passing on problems to other GPs. De-listed patients are referred to the local Family Health Services Authority, which must find them another GP.

Expenses

A worker who has been attacked may incur a number of expenses, for example:

- costs of transport home, to the GP or hospital;
- repair or replacement of damaged clothing;
- costs of dental repair or treatment;
- repair or replacement of spectacles or watch broken in the incident;

- prescription charges;
- repair of damage to the worker's car.

Formal agreement about a policy on reimbursement of expenses will avoid the need for *ad hoc* decisions, and the possibility of inconsistent or unfair decision-making.

Protected earnings

Any employee who has to take time off work will be likely to be concerned about loss of earnings, either as a direct result of being off work for a long time or indirectly because, although paid their wage or salary, they miss out on bonus or overtime payments.

Reasonable employers would generally take the view that employees who suffer violence in the line of duty should not suffer financially as well. How employers manage the problems of earnings will very much depend on the particular circumstances and systems for payments within the organization. In cases where a straightforward monthly salary or weekly wage is paid this could simply be guaranteed. Where bonus payments or overtime are involved it may be necessary to work out an average over a period before the incident and guarantee it per month or per week while the employee is off work.

Unlike the case of time off work, it may well be better to have a very clear policy on protecting earnings so that it can be communicated to all employees and they can know exactly what to expect. A policy also avoids the risk of any unfair treatment based on judgements that would have to be made in an *ad hoc* system.

Legal help

The sort of legal help an employee may require will depend on the nature of the violent incident and the consequences of it. In some cases the police will bring a prosecution, and while this has the advantage of costing the employee nothing directly, he/she may get nothing in the form of compensation from it. There could be costs attached if the employee is to give evidence, and the organization could help with this and/or make good any loss of property or goods. In addition, information and support from a legal department or solicitor conversant with the proceedings could help the employee in the potentially traumatic business of giving evidence.

When the police do not bring a prosecution there may still be scope for the individual to bring a civil action. In the first instance the organization could secure legal advice on behalf of the employee as to whether or not a civil action is likely to be successful in the circumstances. Bringing a civil action can be very costly, and organizations should consider to what extent they can assist in bringing such actions, in what circumstances, and the terms of such an arrangement.

In the UK, where personal injuries have been sustained that are directly attributable to a crime of violence, application can be made for an award from the Criminal Injuries Compensation Board (who administer the Criminal Injury Compensation Scheme). The procedures are complex and organizations could offer help and advice, through legal departments or their solicitors, to employees who wish to make an application.

Insurance

Employers should carry insurance to cover the death or injury of an employee as a result of assault in the course of employment. Care is needed to ensure that GPs carry sufficient insurance cover for themselves and their employees.

Accommodation

It is wise to consider the possibility that employees may be threatened with violence in or against their homes if patients know where they live. Safety procedures should deal with the issue of giving out telephone numbers, or details of where a member of staff lives, but even with these precautions a determined and threatening patient may discover where a health professional lives.

This sort of situation is likely to be rare, but where a worker has been threatened, and there is a serious danger of attack or repeat attack, it may be necessary for alternative accommodation to be provided for the employee and his/her family for a short time – perhaps until the attacker has been arrested and charged, and the assessed danger has passed. Many health care organizations have access to residential premises, and it is worth considering establishing a 'safe house' for use should these very exceptional circumstances arise.

Other staff

Where a member of staff has been subjected to violence, their colleagues will have a range of reactions. Some may become very anxious about the danger of violent attacks. It is helpful to involve colleagues in a review of safety procedures, soon after the incident and again in six to eight months' time, when initial shocked reaction may have given way to a more relaxed – and possibly complacent – attitude towards personal safety.

Guidelines for colleagues

If someone has experienced violence, whether or not they have been away from work, other staff can be helped to react appropriately if given some guidelines, for example:

- Our natural curiosity can get the better of us at times; staff should be asking 'How are you?' rather than 'What happened?'
- By all means show concern for your colleague, but be aware that he/she may not be ready or able to discuss feelings or the incident.
- If your colleague does want to talk, let them; also let them be in control of what they tell you. Ask questions sensitively, and do not probe if they are reticent.
- When he/she wants to stop talking, do not persist.
- Do not criticize the action your colleague describes taking or not taking in the incident.
- If you are at all concerned about your colleague, suggest someone with training to whom they should speak; if you do not believe they can do this but are sure they need help, you should speak to someone yourself, for example a line manager or personnel staff.

Part 2

Guidelines for health care workers

Training, knowledge and forethought help people to develop confidence and achieve personal control. The following guidelines are designed to help individuals in avoiding and managing violence, in a variety of working situations in the clinic, surgery or hospital and away from the normal workplace.

14 Interviewing techniques

Health care professionals, and other care workers, are regularly involved in conducting interviews on sensitive issues. It is remarkable how few professional training courses include a component on interpersonal skills, on interview techniques, and on dealing with difficult situations.

Complaints from patients are often as much concerned with the manner in which their concerns have been dealt with, as with the actual medical treatment which they have received. It is suggested in *Violence at Work*[1] that 'in order to diffuse violence, the communication skills of doctors need to be addressed and enhanced'. Several ways of doing this are suggested:

- '• Looking at the undergraduate curriculum of medical students and providing training and role-plays in the communication training module of the basic care curriculum.
- • Postgraduate education should address the problems of professionals in dealing with violence within their work setting – for example, hospital or general practice. Training courses should be led by suitably qualified professionals, with regular updates.
- • Training courses with a multi-disciplinary approach may be useful in identifying ways of dealing with violence in a particular work setting.'

The following guidelines will help health professionals to make the most effective use of interviews, and to reduce opportunities for misunderstandings and frustration:

- • Don't try to blind a patient with science; use language they can understand, but don't be condescending or talk down to them.
- • Shake hands and introduce yourself by name; explain who you are, in terms of your job, if they don't already know.
- • If you escort a patient to a room, walk beside them on the level, go in front going upstairs, and walk behind coming downstairs.

103

- If the patient is reacting badly to you for reasons of your sex, age, class and so on, hand them over to someone else with their agreement.
- If you know a patient has been aggressive or violent in the past, find out about the incident if possible; it may help you to plan for and manage your interview with them.
- Beware if you are told of previous aggression and violence; it could be exaggerated and adversely affect your approach to an interview.
- Think about your clothing. Obviously your dress and appearance is up to you, but you may wish to consider avoiding:

  - ties, blouses with ties, necklaces and so on that could be used to strangle;
  - earrings that can be pulled or torn off;
  - long hair that can be caught;
  - shoes that mean you can't run if you need to.

- Think about your position in relation to the interviewee:

  - seats of equal height;
  - seats at a 45-degree angle are less threatening; opposite implies confrontation; side-by-side, cooperation;
  - you may want a desk between you and the patient for safety, but it could also form a barrier;
  - aggressive or violent people have a wider than normal buffer zone and may need more space.

- Think about taking notes to show you are taking the patient seriously, but make sure they do not suspect a lack of interest on your part, or that you are compiling a secret dossier of some sort. This can also help in keeping appropriate levels of eye contact.
- If you are both standing, try to be relaxed; match your position with the patient's.
- Do not stand over a seated patient: it gives the impression of crowding, superiority or greater power.
- Try to calm aggression by using sympathy, empathy, and paraphrasing what was said to show you understand.
- Try to solve problems immediately, if only minor ones – to demonstrate you are helping and trying to find solutions.
- Depersonalize issues: if you are governed by rules of some sort, explain that and the limits of your discretion.
- On the other hand, presenting yourself as a person rather than an official can help, especially if you can convey the upset or hurt that abuse or aggression causes you personally.
- Avoid provocative expressions such as 'calm down', 'don't be silly'.
- More calming approaches include *'we'* (share the problem) in 'the

position *we* are in ... ', '*we* need to ... ', or '*we* can tackle it in this way ... '
- Don't make promises you can't keep.
- Never get drawn into aggression – do not use insults, swear, threaten or ridicule.
- Don't set deadlines such as 'if you don't stop in two minutes I'll leave' – you may not be able to keep them, or you may irritate the patient.
- Listen, and show you are listening by nodding; expressions such as 'yes' and 'I see' indicate attention too.
- Adopt a relaxed posture – open, rather than a closed, arms-folded approach.
- Avoid tapping pens, fiddling with anything or doodling.
- If the situation is escalating, try taking a break; the change may help defuse things. You could simply stretch your legs or go for a cup of tea or change venue.

Recognizing and avoiding danger

Physical well-being

Your physical well-being can have a significant impact on your safety, quite apart from its influence on your ability to take evasive action should this become necessary. Health care professionals, although advising others on health matters, can easily become stressed themselves.

Many health care professionals neglect their own physical and emotional health. If you are unfit, overtired or stressed you are less likely to have the energy and attention to put into ensuring your own safety. You may become less able to deal with difficult people or situations, or more prone to escalate difficult situations into dangerous ones. Think about aspects of your physical well-being: learn to recognize when you are feeling down, sluggish or over-tired and start looking after yourself. For example:

- Eat properly – have a sensible, varied, balanced diet. Eat regularly and take time to eat meals. Avoid too much fat, sugar and stimulants such as alcohol.
- Exercise – take regular, daily exercise, such as a brisk walk, a daily swim, or get an exercise machine. Half an hour a day can make a big difference.
- Sleep well – make sure you allow yourself the sleep you need. Relax before going to bed, have a bath, read or have a soothing drink, but avoid alcohol or sleeping pills.
- Relax – take up a hobby that is relaxing, and learn yoga or meditation. Make time to go out and do things and be with people. Set a time each

day to listen to music, lie on a sunbed or pamper yourself by doing
something you want to do.

Messages you give

Consider how other people perceive you and the messages which you give
to them. Do you appear confident, assured, pleasant and competent? Are
you likely to be perceived as nervous, uneasy, uncomfortable or unsure?

Much research into the types of people who are attacked suggests that the
messages we give can have an effect on the likelihood, or otherwise, of being
the subject of other people's violence. People who convey by their posture,
movement, demeanour and behaviour that they are confident are less likely
to be attacked. Some ways of conveying self-assurance and confidence
include:

- Stand tall and straight, rather than hunched.
- Walk steadily, maintaining a rhythm rather than stumbling along.
- Keep your head up; look ahead, not down.
- Pay attention to your surroundings: if you look alert and aware you are
  less vulnerable, but avoid looking around shyly or nervously.
- Know where you are going; avoid looking lost or disorientated.
- Avoid eye contact with other people.
- Look calm and serious, as if knowing what you are about and in
  control.
- Avoid giving the impression of being tense or nervous by wringing
  your hands, fidgeting or fiddling.
- Keep yourself balanced by placing your weight evenly on both feet;
  you will look and feel steady and secure.

Awareness of others

Like everyone else, you will have first impressions of people or make certain
assumptions about them. These impressions and assumptions are very
immediate; they may be right or wrong, and may change or not as you inter-
act with the other person. These impressions and assumptions can sometimes help you to make judgements about your own safety and help you
avoid danger.

In some ways it does not matter if you are right or wrong or doing an
injustice to the other person because, for your own safety, it is as well not to
wait to find out how accurate or fair you are. For example, a woman walking
on her own at night may see a group of apparently drunken youths
approaching and feel threatened. They may be very nice young lads having
a good time, but they may not. The wisest action is probably to assume the

worst and change direction. Your impressions and assumptions can be based on prejudices and generalizations that bear little resemblance to reality. The consequences can be that your behaviour towards people (body language, voice, eye contact, manner) based on those assumptions, prejudices or stereotypes can trigger aggressive or violent reactions. This is particularly true if the other person is ill at ease because of being in your 'territory', is upset for some reason, has come with feelings of frustration to make a complaint, or believes they are set for a battle with bureaucracy in order to have their needs met.

The sorts of behaviour that can trigger aggressive or violent reactions could include, for example:

- talking down to people; patronizing them;
- telling people they are wrong to feel the way they do;
- standing on your official dignity;
- trivializing people's concern, upset, frustration, problem;
- using the wrong form of address or the wrong name;
- using certain words or phrases;
- expressing assumptions (for example, 'women can't understand computers');
- ridicule;
- using organizational jargon.

Think about the way you behave towards other people. Are there things that you do that may trigger unwanted reactions? Can you assess your own behaviour, or would it be helpful to ask others for feedback about how you are received? Do you ever try to put yourself in the other person's place and imagine what or how they may be feeling, so you can gauge appropriate responses?

Empathy

There is a tendency to focus on ourselves in situations that are difficult or threatening, because of our bodily reactions, but it is important and helpful to try to think about the other person too.

If you are working in any environment that involves people – especially one which provides a service, dealing with people's problems or any sort of enforcement – you are likely to face difficult interpersonal situations at some time. When people are upset, annoyed or frustrated they are not necessarily in control of themselves or as rational as normal. If they become violent it is quite possible for the person on the receiving end of their behaviour to make matters worse by becoming annoyed or responding inappropriately. While this is understandable, it is not very helpful.

When faced with a violent person, try to avoid becoming irritated or angry yourself: empathize with the other person. Accept the way they perceive the situation (even if they have the wrong end of the stick), acknowledge their feelings are real (even though they may not be reasonable) and allow that, given their starting point, their behaviour is appropriate – it certainly is to them. In other words, put yourself in their shoes and imagine how you might behave. This is a first step in helping you to start from the same point as the other person. If you can establish what they think, believe has happened, are feeling and so on, it can be much easier to understand why they are upset or angry and avoid the personal responses of feeling accused or becoming angry yourself.

This approach means you can avoid approaching the situation feeling that you must defend yourself, prove the other person wrong, or win. It should not be a win–lose but a win–win situation. To achieve this you need to be able to acknowledge two different starting points, the aims of the two people, and work out a process to achieve a compromise or solution that will satisfy (not necessarily totally) both parties.

Unfortunately, many situations degenerate into lose–lose situations of violence, where all parties end up dissatisfied or hurt because no one thinks about trying to see the situation from the other side: they are too busy reacting.

Signs and signals

Someone who is potentially violent can give off signs and signals that constitute a recognizable warning. If you are out and about travelling there are some very obvious warning signs that should alert you to possible danger – for example, if people are:

- following you;
- lurking in corners;
- shouting at you;
- making comments;
- high on drink or drugs;
- staring at you;
- trying to catch your eye;
- trying to make conversation.

In circumstances where you are actively interacting with other people you should look for signs that indicate potential or impending violence, such as:

- agitation;
- tapping the table;
- loud speech/shouting;

- muscle tension in face, hands, limbs;
- fidgeting, hand-wringing;
- clenching fists;
- drawing breath in sharply;
- colour of face – pale could indicate danger: the body is ready for action; a red face is likely to indicate a bark worse than bite, but it could change;
- finger-wagging or -jabbing;
- inability to be still – even pacing about;
- swearing;
- staring eyes;
- sweating;
- oversensitivity to ideas, suggestions;
- rapid mood swings.

When assessing the risk of violence in a situation you are in or about to enter, ask yourself questions, such as:

- Does the person have

    - a history of violence?
    - criminal convictions for violence?
    - a history of psychiatric illness causing violence?
    - a medical condition which may result in loss of self-control?

- Has the person

    - verbally abused me in the past?
    - threatened me with violence before?
    - attacked me before?
    - abused, threatened or attacked colleagues before?

- Is the person likely

    - to be dealing with high levels of stress?
    - to be drunk?
    - to be on drugs?

- Could the person see me as a threat

    - to their liberty?
    - to their family?
    - to them personally?
    - to their business or work?
    - to them getting what they want?

- Has the person got

- realistic and reasonable expectations of what I can do for them?
- an impression of me as unhelpful or unwilling?

Ask also:

- Do I feel confident to handle the situation?
- Have I got back-up?
- Can I summon help?
- Have I got a plan of how to approach the situation?

Awareness of the environment

Being aware of the environment can help you recognize potential risks and ways of avoiding them. To do this you need to take positive and active notice of your surroundings. 'Environment' here means the physical environment around you in the workplace, travelling on business or working in others' homes and premises, and the nature of the organization within which you work. Taking notice of your physical environment means taking notice of what and who is around you, including:

- **Access** – who can get in, where and how?
- **Egress** – how can you get out: exits, escape routes, routes to well-lit or populated areas?
- **Isolation** – can you make contact with others, see them or be seen?
- **Alarms** – how can you raise an alarm or summon help?
- **Lighting** – at night especially: is your route, car park, meeting place and so on well-lit?
- **Hiding places** – are there corners or places not properly visible or badly-lit, where people could hide?
- **Situations** – are you likely to be affected by pub closing time, football crowds or other situations when you may be more at risk?
- **Locations** – are you conscious of areas of higher risk in the town or city or particularly risky locations such as gardens, parks, underpasses, alleyways, and so on?
- **Weapons** – are there things around you that could be used as weapons by others, or present danger?
- **Precautions** – are you aware of the physical forms of protection available to you, and do you, or could you, use them properly?
- **People** – do you take notice of other people around you, where they are and what they are doing, so that you could recognize a risk, such as being followed or watched?

Awareness of the nature of the agency you work in means being conscious of what it is you do and the risks inherent in it, for example:

- Is there general public access to your place of work?
- Does your work require you to deal directly with the public?
- Are the public you may deal with likely to present problems because of the purpose of their visit, such as complaints?
- Are you likely to be exposed to people who present a risk because they are ill, drunk or on drugs – for example, in a hospital or hostel?
- Does your work involve you in tasks that may not be popular or could lead to a disagreement, such as inspection or enforcement?
- Are you potentially a target because you transport or collect money or valuables?
- Does your work involve being in others' homes or premises where you may be more or less welcome?
- Do you travel on professional business or work away from a base and thus become isolated?

Awareness of the working environment is the key to spotting risks and possible dangers so that these can then be minimized by adopting safe working practices.

Reference

1 Schneider, V. and Maguire, J. (1993), *Violence at Work and its Impact on the Medical Profession Within Hospitals and the Community*, London: British Medical Association, September.

15 Non-verbal communication

Incidents of violence in the workplace are very often considered to be occasions when communication of any 'normal' sort has broken down. However, it is important to remember that the violent person is, or started out by, trying to communicate. The reason that communication has broken down may not be solely that an individual is prone to violence; it may be a result of all sorts of messages they, and others in the situation, are picking up.

As much as 90 per cent of communication is through non-verbal behaviour, so learning to read the non-verbal signs and signals can be invaluable when trying to assess situations for risk, in predicting violent outbursts and in presenting yourself.

The components of communication are often described as follows:

- verbal – representing 7 per cent of communication;
- non-verbal – vocal tone, which makes up about 38 per cent of communication;
- non-verbal – body language, which makes up 55 per cent of communication.

Very many different elements of verbal and non-verbal behaviour are at play in communication. People give and receive signals, whether consciously or not, and these signals can trigger a spectrum of responses from positive to negative.

Recognizing signals

Knowledge of the elements of non-verbal communication can help you to develop effective communication skills by enabling you to:

113

- recognize danger signals from others;
- avoid stereotypical or snap judgements of other people that could trigger violence;
- be conscious that other people will receive signals from you and form impressions;
- choose to send certain signals and messages through your non-verbal behaviour.

Impressions and stereotypes

On meeting someone, or even speaking to them on the telephone, we have an immediate impression of them. Generally speaking, we do not notice individual physical aspects of the person straight away (for example, eyes, hair); we are more likely to register their age, gender and race. It is all too easy to make snap judgements of people on the basis of first impressions and our own stereotypes.

Because of a person's colour, age or disability (we rarely see the ability) it is easy to make judgements about capability, to respond stereotypically to questions or requests, or to prejudge that person's behaviour. Others will also respond to us in this way, gaining a first impression or pigeon-holing us as a result of their stereotypes.

It is important to acknowledge that we all have first impressions and work from the basis of stereotypes. It is equally important to remember that they may be totally inaccurate or irrelevant. Our 'norm' is not necessarily the other person's 'norm', and it is therefore easy to misinterpret the signs and signals.

Avoiding the possibly unproductive – or even unsafe – consequences of this means putting stereotypes to one side, difficult though it is, and allowing people time to make themselves known to us before we make any decisions about them.

This approach needs to be balanced, however, with recognition that 'instinct' should not be ignored. There are occasions when, without it being quite clear why this is the case, instinct tells us to be cautious about a particular person. This has been referred to as the 'hairs on the back of the neck' response. Where there is a strong feeling of unease, this should be respected, and caution exercised.

Dress   Many of our snap judgements about people are as a consequence of dress. We tend to make assessments on the basis of:

- smart or scruffy;
- formal or casual;
- appropriate or inappropriate;
- old-fashioned or trendy.

We also tend to react on the basis of what we like, or our past experiences; for example, a uniform can be reassuring or threatening. Our assessment of the person is entirely subjective, and may or may not be accurate or anything like the perception the other person has of him/herself.

What is smart to one person is old-fashioned to another, and what is practical and appropriate to one may be scruffy or too casual to another. How we dress is clearly our own choice, unless our job demands specific clothing and we accept that condition of employment. However, like it or not, we must remember that our dress will have an impact on other people and their perceptions of us. We all have to make decisions about whether or not to choose clothing with that in mind, and decide whether we want to try to create a particular impression.

Wearing certain types of clothing can convey a relaxed, open, welcoming appearance, mark the person as 'one of the crowd', or send out signals that the person is businesslike, but there is no guarantee that we will always create the impression we wish.

For example, going into an organization with a serious complaint, a customer may be faced with a very smartly dressed, besuited woman trained to smile and deal with complaints efficiently. The visitor may see an over-dressed individual, grinning as if all were well when plainly, to the complainant, it is not.

Not everyone will be able or willing to take time or make the effort to go beyond first impressions, particularly if they are upset, annoyed or angry to start with. They may also be predisposed to misread signals from others. The appropriateness of clothing is thus important: people can be helped to relate more readily to others if they are not surprised or confused by the signals sent out. It is up to individuals to decide to what extent they will accommodate the expectations of other people and the context in which they are relating to them.

The issue of dressing safely is a contentious one, particularly for women. Certainly women should be free to choose what they wear, but it is essential to bear in mind that the intended messages may not be the ones that are received by other people. Although it curtails individual freedom, a decision to dress differently may be essential to minimize risk.

It is not just clothes themselves that convey messages to others. Carrying a briefcase or clipboard can be seen as efficient, or officious; wearing badges or insignia (including the old school tie!) can bring recognition and acceptance, or aversion.

Eye contact Appropriate eye contact is a very important element of communication. If you look at someone constantly you will soon find that they become uncomfortable. People do not generally like to be stared at, peered at or be the subject of a penetrating gaze. Too much eye contact can be interpreted as being threatening or overbearing, and can trigger aggressive responses. Too little eye contact may lead people to believe that you are not listening to them, not paying attention or not taking them seriously, and can also lead to an aggressive reaction.

Appropriate eye contact, for the vast majority of people, means keeping it regular but not constant. A speaker will look away from a listener, but will establish direct eye contact from time to time to see that the listener is attentive, is understanding what is being said, to pick up clues about the listener's reactions and to modify what is being said if necessary.

A listener makes eye contact to demonstrate attentiveness and understanding, but can also convey discomfort or confusion, boredom or other reactions to the speaker. People's eyes can be extremely expressive and show humour, fear, distress, shyness, excitement, and so on. Eye contact enables us to pick up these signals, and, in combination with other signals, realize how we are affecting the other person or assess how well we are communicating. This allows us to modify our behaviour and to recognize changes in the other person on which we may choose to, or need to, act.

You can learn to convey certain messages by practising in front of a mirror and using your eyes to express what you want. This can be useful in difficult situations because you can avoid being 'given away' by your eyes when you have learnt to adopt a calm, steady look and can maintain regular eye contact even under stress.

Facial expressions   Our facial expressions can convey a great deal about the way we are thinking and feeling. Eyes and mouths are probably the most expressive features, and can show feelings on our faces that we are denying with our words.

Facial expressions show everything from terror to total calm, and they can change very quickly as our thoughts and feelings change. Reading people's facial expressions can help in recognizing when they are upset, angry or annoyed, even if their words are not expressing these feelings.

It is often possible to see tension or anger building up on someone's face long before they express it verbally, so you can be forewarned of possible danger and take appropriate action.

Your facial expression may also betray feelings that you would prefer to keep to yourself, or you may wish to learn to recognize and adopt particular facial expressions in certain circumstances. You can learn about your own expressions by sitting in front of a mirror and practising looking tense, relaxed, upset, calm, angry and so on, so that you come to recognize the feeling of each and can learn to adopt expressions that will help you when communicating with others.

Body posture/movement   Posture and body movements can convey an enormous range of messages about how a person is feeling, their mood, their attitudes and how they are relating to others. Sometimes the messages are intended, such as a wave, while sometimes they are not, like nervous fiddling in an interview.

Gestures and movements also have acquired meanings that are understood generally – such as 'thumbs up' – or by particular groups – such as secret signs of a gang of children. Some gestures and movements have meaning in one society or culture and no meaning, or a different meaning, in others. Staff who work with people from a range of ethnic backgrounds, for example, need to be aware of cultural and religious issues which will affect communication.

In some cases posture, gestures or movements may have simply become habits, and are not intended to convey anything, though other people may still read meaning into them. While observing and endeavouring to understand the messages given by posture and body movements is important in communication, it is also necessary to remember how easy it can be to misread or misinterpret the messages. Sometimes it is as well to check your understanding by asking the other person how they feel or what they are thinking. Some of the ways in which people may convey messages through posture and body movements are as follows:

- **Anxious**
    - clenched hands;
    - pulling at clothing;
    - fiddling with hair, pen and so on;
    - fidgeting, changing position;
    - frowning;
    - biting lips.

- **Depressed**
    - slumped in a chair;
    - downcast;
    - shoulders hunched;
    - not responding;
    - over-the-top bright and breezy manner.

- **Disapproving**
    - pulling away;
    - folded arms;
    - stiff, upright, looking down;
    - raised eyebrows.

- **Frustrated**

  - sighing;
  - eyes raised skywards;
  - shaking of head;
  - jerky movements of hands, such as tapping.

- **Aggressive**

  - clenched fists or flexing hands;
  - finger-wagging or -jabbing;
  - shaking of head;
  - arm-waving;
  - rigid posture, tense muscles.

- **Threatened**

  - closed posture, arms folded, legs crossed;
  - averted gaze, head turned away;
  - backing away.

- **Relaxed**

  - open posture, arms at side;
  - smiling, head up and making eye contact;
  - flowing movements, not jerky or sudden.

Learning to read the messages given by posture and body movements can help you to recognize how other people are feeling and reacting in the course of communication. You can then make decisions about your own behaviour that may increase the effectiveness of communication by relaxing, calming or reassuring the other person. If the messages you receive are danger signals then you can respond in the most appropriate way to keep yourself safe by defusing the aggression, getting help or getting away.

You can also learn about your own posture and body movements by observing yourself; video is effective for this. You may decide to avoid certain habits of behaviour that convey messages you do not wish to convey. For example, many of us point or wave fingers in excitement or to add weight to what we are saying. Our listeners may well perceive the gesture as aggressive or overbearing.

You could also learn behaviour that will be helpful in certain circum-stances. For example, you can learn how to hold yourself and what to do with your hands to avoid appearing nervous and fidgeting in difficult situa-tions, such as interviews or when someone is complaining to you.

Reading the messages in posture and body movement is a skill that can be learnt and applied, but care must be taken to avoid reading too much into what you observe or assuming you are always correct in your reading. Cultural differences, regional differences, individual habits and your own approach, preferences and attitudes all complicate the process, so check your understanding with the other person.

Space Communication between people can be very significantly affected by the way in which the space around them, and what they consider to be their space, is treated by others.

Personal space Each of us has around us a zone of personal space; for some people the zone is very large and for others it is only small. The zone can vary too, depending on the individual's mood at any particular time. It can feel very offensive or aggressive if someone comes too close and invades this invisible buffer zone. Of course loved ones and close friends are welcomed into the personal space, but others may not be. The invasion of personal space by strangers can feel very threatening, create tension or lead to upset or anger.

If someone invades your personal space you are likely to want to back away and re-establish the space between you; if the person follows, you may end up feeling pursued or cornered. On the other hand, too much distance between two people trying to communicate can seem like a gulf, and make each feel as if the other is unapproachable or inaccessible.

Getting the balance right means being very sensitive to the other person's signals so that you can be close enough to avoid feelings of distance without intruding on their personal space. You will often find that you can get physically closer to someone standing up without causing discomfort than you can sitting down; people generally seem to require a larger buffer zone when seated.

Spatial relationship Just as the distance between yourself and another person is important, so is the relationship, or orientation, in space. Sitting side by side with another person is usually recognized as a cooperative relationship where you are working together as equals. Sitting opposite someone can seem authoritarian, official, formal, competitive or, especially when a desk is used, as putting up barriers. Seats at an angle of 45 degrees are less threatening. When in a group, sitting in a circle can signal that everyone has an equal, if different, contribution to make.

Sitting in rows in a formal setting tends to put the power in the hands of a leader and leave it there, and makes getting to know people and forming relationships more difficult. The height at which people sit is significant too: try to ensure you sit at the same height as the person you are talking to. A higher position tends to signal a hierarchy in the relationship, even if this is not intended.

Territory   Another form of space around us is territory. It is a wider area or place that we regard as ours and as where we belong: perhaps a room at home, our office, or the area around our desk at work. Our expectation is that, as ours, this territory will be respected and not invaded by others. We are all likely to react adversely if we find someone going through our things, using our things or otherwise invading the territory.

When jobs entail working in other people's homes or premises – particularly where this involves inspection, enforcement or other duties that may be unwelcome – it is not unusual to find that people can become violent. Part of the reaction may well be because their territory is invaded and they have little or no power to prevent it. If you are entering other people's territory it is important to realize that there may be adverse reactions, so take sensible precautions, such as not going alone where there is cause for concern.

Touch   As part of communication, touch has an important role in showing love, support, concern, empathy, encouragement and so on, as well as the simpler purposes, such as greeting with a handshake, or a congratulatory pat on the back.

The acceptability of different kinds of touch varies between individuals, cultures and other groups, and we learn what is appropriate and what is not through observation, experience and reading the signals we receive from others. Some people will not like to be touched at all; they may be distressed by it or feel threatened, and could react aggressively. Some people feel unable to touch because they are unsure of how it will be received, or it may seem 'unprofessional' in some settings, or 'sloppy'. Others, however, are uninhibited and spontaneous about touching. There are also people who may well want the comfort or reassurance of touch but may be unable to signal that this is what they need.

Medical examination and routine involves touching the patient, but touch generally is an area requiring careful consideration of the other person's needs. It can be patronizing, offensive, feel like an invasion of personal space or even recall unpleasant and traumatic memories. On the other hand, touch can be the most effective way of showing genuine care and concern for another person and establishing a bond with them.

One way to discover if touch is needed and welcome is to observe the other person carefully while offering limited support, such as a hand on their arm. They will signal their comfort or discomfort and you can decide whether to move away or put a comforting arm around their shoulders.

Voice   In communication, what is most important may not be what you say but the way that you say it, or hear it. Tone of voice, pitch, speed, rhythm and accent can all play a part in the communication process over and above the words. To communicate effectively you should avoid the following:

- making assumptions about people because of their accent;
- making assumptions based on nationality or race; people may sound excited because English is their second language, and this does not mean they are necessarily dangerous;
- lapsing into a clinical or detached response to people where your voice has little tone or rhythm and you convey disinterest or boredom;
- letting your tension get the better of you and betraying your feelings because your voice becomes higher-pitched, you adopt an excited tone or start to gabble;
- adopting a supercilious tone, as there is little more likely to trigger a violent reaction than the other person feeling put down, foolish or wrong;
- mumbling or speaking too quickly, because being unable to hear properly or follow what is said is irritating and frustrating to the listener;
- showing your views and feelings in your tone (for example, contempt or sarcasm) but *not* in your words; the listener is still more than likely to pick up your signals and respond in kind.

In dealing with others, watch for the following:

- raised voice, rapid speech and gabbling, as this may signal rising tension;
- changes in tone and pitch as the conversation progresses that may suggest anger, frustration or impending violent behaviour;
- slow, menacing tones that, despite the words themselves, demonstrate that the speaker is angry and likely to erupt into violent behaviour.

One of the most useful of skills is to be able to control your voice in difficult or threatening situations. Tension caused by fear of real or perceived problems can raise your pitch or even make it difficult to speak coherently. If you gently sigh, expelling all the air, you will release the tension, regain voice control and be in the position to react with confidence. Your aim is to be calm, clear, firm and polite, even if the other person is none of these things. You can practice this using a tape recorder to get accustomed to your own voice and to try out and learn calm, clear, firm and polite responses. Another way is to work with other people and role-play situations so that you can practise responding appropriately.

Listening   Listening is an essential part of communicating effectively. It can be passive, but to be really effective it needs to be – and be seen to be – active. On the one hand, active listening implies letting the speaker know you are listening and following what is said by sounds you make ('mmm, yes') and the gestures or feedback (nodding your head, smiling acknowl-edgement) you use. This confirms for the speaker that you are attentive. On the other hand, active listening is about the process of picking up non-verbal signals, assessing the messages in and behind words, and putting all the non-verbal information together with the verbal to build up a complete picture of what is being said.

Listening actively to someone can be very important, first of all to them, because:

- it shows they are being given the space to say what they want to say;
- they are being given time and attention by someone;
- it demonstrates that what they say is felt to be worth listening to;
- it avoids feelings of being fobbed off, frustration and anger.

It is important also to you, because:

- it allows you to focus attention on that person and nothing else;
- you can concentrate on both the verbal and non-verbal communication together, and form a more accurate view of the problem or issue and the person's feelings;
- it avoids misunderstanding or partial understanding, and so can save time and problems;
- it makes it possible to respond sensibly and sensitively to the other person;
- it gives you a better chance of predicting behaviour that may put you at risk.

Making time to listen actively to someone can help establish a relationship and cooperation. Someone who has been listened to and feels they have been heard is more likely to accept a less than ideal solution to a problem than someone who feels they have not had a chance to explain or been given explanations in return.

16 Coping with violence

No matter how aware and careful you are, how skilful you are at recognizing and avoiding danger, or how well you implement calming or controlling techniques, you could still find yourself faced with violent behaviour.

There is a very fine line between someone being upset, angry or giving vent to their feelings, and violence directed at another person. The recipient will, to some extent, determine where that line is drawn, depending on the point at which they personally feel at risk, threatened or unsafe. In this chapter we consider possible responses to violent behaviour not involving physical attack, and then responses to physical violence itself.

Violence not involving physical attack

If someone becomes abusive and threatening, consider whether or not you can cope with the situation. You should not feel you have to cope with it alone: you can seek help from other people or leave altogether. First keep calm, relax, allow yourself time to think and decide the best course of action. Ask yourself if what has occurred so far in the exchange means that someone else, especially briefed by you, would be better placed to handle the situation.

Colleagues may have particular skills or experience that you do not have. The situation may be such that it requires specialist help, such as security or the police to eject a person; if so, you should get the help quickly before the situation deteriorates.

If you decide you can cope, there are a number of different approaches. One that has been found to work well is the 'control trilogy'. It has three stages: calming, reaching and controlling. Each of them is dealt with here in turn.

Calming

The purpose of the calming stage is to take the heat out of the situation and enable you to start communicating with the other person positively. The principle is simply to accept what is said, not evaluate it or respond to it at this stage.

Remember that people can hyperventilate under stress. Calm yourself first, breathe *out* first and then breathe steadily while releasing the tension in your muscles. If you find this difficult, tense your muscles still further and then release them – this can be very effective.

Think about yourself, particularly your verbal and non-verbal communication:

- **Voice** – keep your voice steady and calm; maintain an even tone and pitch. Speak gently, slowly, clearly and carefully.
- **Face** – show that you are listening and attentive; use nods to signal you are following. Try to relax your facial muscles and convey openness and empathy with the speaker.
- **Eyes** – make eye contact, but avoid constant eye contact that may be threatening or trigger aggression because it is perceived as staring.
- **Position** – try to avoid eyeball-to-eyeball positions or positions where you are higher than the other person. Avoid barriers, too, if it is safe to do so.
- **Posture** – avoid aggressive or defensive stances, such as arms folded, hands on hips, or waving fingers or arms. Try to look relaxed and open.
- **Space** – give the aggressor plenty of space. When we are upset or angry the personal space buffer zone we require can be greater than normal, and the proximity of others more threatening.

Now think about the other person; do things and encourage them to do things that will contribute to calming them, such as:

- **Talking** – keep the aggressor talking and explaining the problem, their perception of what has happened, why they feel aggrieved and so on. Use verbal and non-verbal prompts (saying 'mmm' or 'yes', or nodding) to keep them talking. Use open questions to encourage them to talk, explain or even think out loud. All this uses up energy and helps to get pent-up frustration out of their system.
- **Listen** – make sure you listen: the information you gather may be useful. Make sure they know you are listening to them. Listen also for the feelings, concerns and possible intentions behind their words.
- **Hear them out** – let this calming phase go on as long as necessary so that the aggressor feels the whole story has been told and heard. Also

hear them out from the point of view of not drawing any conclusions or trying to assess, evaluate or solve the problems at this stage. Concentrate on the aggressor and what is being said; this is their space and they will be doing most of the talking.

- **Watch** – as you go through the calming phase watch for changes in behaviour, for example: lowering of voice to 'normal' tone, relaxing of facial muscles, steadier breathing, change in language used, postural changes or increasing tiredness (being aggressive is tiring). These changes can signal that the aggressor is becoming calmer and more approachable.
- **Resist arguing** – it is very tempting to respond and become engaged in an argument, especially if you are the butt of the aggression or accused in some way. Resist arguing; it is far more likely to result in conflict or confrontation than contribute to defusing the situation.
- **Be yourself** – do not hide behind authority, status or a job title. Try to convey who you are; tell the aggressor your name and ask them their name. By using your name instead of a description of your status you are presenting yourself as another human being. Later it may be important to explain what authority or status you have, to reassure the person that you are in a position to act on their behalf.

Reaching

When you believe that the aggressor has calmed sufficiently (as judged by the changes you observe) you can begin to reach out and try to build bridges to enable communication. You are likely to be talking more at this stage than the calming stage, as you begin to develop a dialogue.

Continue to behave as before but develop the interactions with the aggressor; you will be able to do this much more effectively if you have listened well in the calming stage, for example:

- Explain back to them what you believe they have said, what the problem is or what they require.
- Seek their confirmation of the facts or key points they have made.
- Clarify what action, assistance and so on they require.
- Encourage them into further relaxation by sitting down, if this is possible, and offering them refreshments.
- Try smiling in encouragement and acknowledgement, as it can relax both of you, but do avoid them thinking you find the situation funny.
- Empathize with their feelings, but avoid any behaviour that could be interpreted as patronizing.
- Ask any questions you need to ask, but make sure they know why you need to know.
- Encourage them to relate to you: check that they remember your name,

your job and how you can help them, as they may have forgotten in the heat of the moment.

- Try to move physically alongside the other person if you can and you feel it is safe; this can signal an intention to work towards a solution together.
- Try to find out about the other person, particularly previous contacts or experience of your organization, or other information that may help you deal with the problem.
- Encourage them to ask questions, clarify things or seek information. In replying, keep it simple and straightforward and avoid jargon.
- Consider taking notes if this gives a positive impression of taking the other person seriously or being the first steps towards helping them. Do not take notes if it appears to the other person to be officialdom in action.

Controlling

Once you feel that you have established a reasonably 'normal' mode of communication with the aggressor you can move into the controlling stage. This does not mean you take over and run the show! It means that you can move forward together in a controlled fashion towards a resolution of the problem.

This stage requires you to maintain the calming and reaching behaviour while moving forward to actually tackling the problem. The aim of this process is win–win: both you and the other person achieving a solution that is satisfactory.

As you work with the other person towards the solution, use the following approaches:

- **Set targets for yourselves** – set out what you need to achieve and when (immediately, later, today, by an agreed time) and make sure both of you agree to and understand what you are aiming for.
- **One at a time** – if the situation or problem is complex, tackle each aspect separately. Agree the list of issues you need to work through with the other person.
- **Simple first** – tackle the simpler problems, issues or aspects of the situation first and quickly. Solving parts of the problem or resolving the simpler issues quickly creates a positive atmosphere by demonstrating progress.
- **Complex later** – move on to tackle the more complex aspects of the situation once you have made some progress and are working more effectively together. Try to divide the more complex aspects so that you can tackle them one by one, or agree the steps you need to take and then go through them.

- **Establish reality** – be clear and honest about what you can and cannot do. Explain what is achievable, when, and what is not, and give the reasons; make sure the other person has realistic expectations.
- **The other view** – acknowledge that the other person has their own views and opinions and will want to put, and have heard, their side of the argument or their analysis of the situation. You need to understand them and help them to hear things from your side and understand you.
- **Admit failings** – if you or your organization have failed in some respect or caused a problem, do not try to cover up. Admit where you have gone wrong and start working on putting it right. If the other person has made a mistake, misunderstood or caused the problem, explain this to them without blaming or causing them to feel or appear foolish.
- **Avoid jargon** – steer clear of organizational or bureaucratic jargon that may confuse or provoke the other person. Above all, avoid defending yourself or the organization by using jargon as a shield: you will simply alienate the other person.
- **Offer alternatives** – if the other person's needs cannot be met (or met fully) it may help to offer alternatives. Any alternatives must be realistic and go some way towards meeting the needs. This approach may offer the other person a way out (a win), especially if they have come to realize they were at fault, that their original expectations are unrealistic, or their needs cannot be met as they would wish.
- **Refer to others** – if you cannot solve the problem or meet the needs, there may be others who can. Do not use this approach as an escape route for yourself by passing the problem on. Refer people on only where you believe they can really obtain help, advice or satisfaction. Try to ensure the person to whom you refer is available, agree a meeting if this is appropriate and pass on information that will be needed. If you can only provide details of whom they can approach then provide proper details (name, address, telephone number, and so on) rather than vague directions.
- **Do not hurry** – even if you are busy you really have to make time to see these sorts of situations through. If you do not you may have wasted a great deal of groundwork or, worse still, left yourself or others open to future aggressive behaviour. Do not show you are pushed for time or try to force the situation along more quickly than the other person can go; that may elicit further aggression.
- **Encourage** – if you are making progress together, express your pleasure at it, acknowledge the other person's part in that, and encourage further cooperation. Encourage them also to express their feelings so that you can know if they do actually feel satisfied with a solution or

progress so far, or if they are just going along with it.

- **Contract** – sometimes it will not be possible to solve a problem or deal with all the issues there and then, as you may need time to collect information, research something and so on. Do not leave the other person feeling 'fobbed off'; think about agreeing future action as a sort of contract between you. Set dates to meet, arrange to telephone or say when you will write. Agree what each of you will do. Show that you have a continuing commitment to helping them. If you do make a commitment – keep it.

- **Review** – at the end of the process go back and review what you have achieved, what each of you has agreed to do, any further contact you have agreed or further targets you have set.

The control trilogy is one way of coping with aggressive people. It is not particularly easy but, given time and practice, can help you think through the process of dealing with an aggressor and develop the appropriate skills to manage the situation and keep safe.

You will not always be able to go through the three stages sequentially and tidily. Very often you will find that you move back and forth between stages. As you learn to observe and predict the other person's behaviour you can react by using the techniques or approaches from each stage. For example, you may be working quite well together on a particular problem when, inadvertently, a raw nerve is touched and the other person becomes aggressive again. You may well have to go right back to basics and start calming the situation again before reaching to re-establish communication and, ultimately, cooperation.

If, when faced with aggression, you decide you can cope and start working through this process, remember you can stop at any time if you feel at risk, or you can get help if you need it. Using the control trilogy to deal with an aggressor can be very effective, but it is time-consuming and requires patience. It also requires you to put aside your feelings to some extent and make your goal that of managing the situation and resolving the problem. You may do a marvellous job and still end up feeling shaky, upset or angry yourself. Think about what you need, go and talk your experience through with someone, make sure you report the incident, or ask for more specialist help if you need to.

Finally, do not assume this method will always be appropriate or succeed. Some aggressors are beyond control, particularly if they are ill, drunk or under the influence of drugs, and in some work situations it is essential to remove someone creating a disruption immediately, for example in a hospital, in which case calming the aggressor is not an option.

Physical attack

Violence can take the form of physical attack. The relative rarity of such events does not mean you should not think about and prepare for the possibility. This is particularly true for health care workers who fall within the category of work where the risks are higher. Should someone launch a physical attack on you the options are limited to:

- **Flight** – escaping from the situation at the first suggestion of physical violence.
- **Compromise** – attempting to defuse or manage the situation or come to some sort of compromise by handing over what is wanted and removing the threat of violence.
- **Fight** – fighting back and ultimately fighting free to escape.

Flight and compromise are by far the safest options.

Flight

Getting away is very often the best form of defence, but escape from attack can be more difficult than it sounds. The effect of a surprise attack can be shock that immobilizes you for a time, and once you have recovered the chance to flee is lost. That is why thinking through how to react is worthwhile – it is hoped you will never need it, but it is worth doing, just as lifesaving and first aid are worth learning although you hope you never need them either.

There are some fairly simple things you can do to make it easier to get away should you need to:

- Practise keeping calm through breathing and relaxation exercises so you can think clearly and move when you want to. Concentrate on breathing out, as this releases the tension. In most cases the tension inhibits the joints and blood flow; this can result in jerky, leadened movements and can lead a person to trip or even fall if they try to run away – walking fast is *much* safer.
- Wear shoes you can walk fast in. They need to be the sort of shoes that stay on your feet and are not liable to collapse if you have to increase your speed.
- Wear sensible clothing that allows you to move quickly and run, and that is not easy to grab to hold on to you or to use to restrain you.
- Be realistic – it is almost impossible to kick someone in the groin, and in the attempt you are most likely to unbalance yourself. Similarly,

kicking shins puts you off balance. Do not imagine you could use your fingers or some object to inflict injury, let alone use them to disable others. Scratching faces, poking eyes out and so on does not come naturally to most people. If you attempt it you are also vulnerable to having your hands and arms, or even your weapon, grabbed and used against you.

- Remember that lashing out with a bag, briefcase or umbrella may not be very sensible either, since you could end up off balance, or have your would-be weapon taken from you and used against you.
- Keep your eyes open in whatever environment you find yourself. Train yourself to automatically register exits, escape routes, places where there will be other people, alarm points, and so on.
- Use an alarm close to the attacker's head, but remember that to use it you need to be able to get hold of it quickly. They are very loud and piercing; even though you are unlikely to find people rushing to your aid, an alarm let off in an attacker's ear will be stunning. While the attacker is stunned you can get away quickly.
- Scream and shout as soon as you are able. Your voice can be the first thing to go when you are in a state of fear and shock. You need to prac-tise breathing out deeply, letting oxygen into your system and allow-ing your blood to circulate properly so you can think and act. Breathing out deeply, like a deep sigh, and expelling the air loudly in a bellow has a remarkable effect. When you shout you should shout something clear and significant, such as an order to 'call the police' rather than 'help', which may be interpreted as larking about.
- Don't imagine you can run away with all your possessions. If, for example, you have a suitcase of heavy items, leave it behind.
- Break-away moves can be useful in giving yourself the element of surprise over the attacker and sufficient time to escape. However, you must learn to use them properly and practise them in order to be able to execute them when you want to, safely and effectively. These need to be well taught and practised until they become automatic. Women need to be aware that they can become somewhat uncoordinated once a month.
- Distract your attacker long enough to be able to break free. You need to be sufficiently calm and self-possessed to do this effectively.
- Make it easy for you to hand over belongings or let an attacker take them if necessary. This means carrying only what you must have with you. Keep money, credit cards, cheque cards, valuables and so on in different places if you must carry them at all. It is best to keep some money and your keys on your person if at all possible.

Compromise

Defusing the situation may not be a realistic option if the attacker is hell-bent on doing violence to you, is ill, or is under the influence of alcohol or drugs. However, many attackers are only driven to physical violence as a means to obtain what they want. You could try an initial approach to defuse the immediate circumstances, and then get away:

- **Calm the attacker** – try to buy some time by staying calm, asking questions, talking and so on until help arrives or you can see a means of escape.
- **Refuse to be intimidated** – shouting back, becoming angry or showing confidence may deter some attackers altogether, or at least give you time to run or for help to arrive.
- **Give in** – hand over whatever it is the attacker wants; it is often sensible to throw whatever it is clear of you so the attacker goes for it while you escape. Do not worry about handing over your employer's property: it will be insured and its loss will be far less costly than injury to you.

If you do make any attempts of this kind you must be constantly on your guard as the situation develops. Always use whatever time or space you can create to your advantage by getting further away, near an exit, closer to other people, into the open, to an alarm and so on. Get away just as soon as you can and get help.

Fighting back – fighting free

Standing your ground and taking your chances in a fight really is a last resort – when you cannot avoid it or all else has failed, for example when you are trapped. If you have to fight back the aim should be to achieve any opening so you can escape. Should you ever be in a situation where you feel you must fight off an attacker, the legal position is complex. You need to remember that:

- You can defend yourself, but may do only what is reasonable in the circumstances. The law permits you to defend yourself, but not to take revenge upon your attacker or to use unreasonable force; such action could be construed as assault, as could hitting out at an attacker leaving the scene.
- You may use force to defend your property, again provided the degree of force is reasonable given the circumstances.
- You may use reasonable force to detain an attacker until help or the police arrive.
- You cannot carry an offensive weapon in a public place even if you

only ever intend to use it in your own defence (Section 1, Prevention of Crime Act 1953). There is no such thing as a defensive weapon. You cannot, therefore, carry anything designed to cause injury, and that includes articles that originally had innocent purposes but have been adapted. Note also that *any* article is an offensive weapon if the bearer intends to use it to cause injury. Special legislation applies to articles with blades or sharp points (Section 139, Criminal Justice Act 1988). It is an offence to carry in a public place an article which has a blade or sharp point, except a folding pocket knife with a blade cutting edge of three inches or less. But if such an article, including a folding pocket knife, were made, adapted or intended to cause injury it would become an offensive weapon.

- The law does not preclude the use of innocent items for self-protection provided that the force used is reasonable. Examples include umbrellas, handbags and walking sticks. Remember, though, that your 'weapon' could be taken from you and used against you. By swinging a bag at your attacker you may be simultaneously presenting your assailant with the booty and a weapon with which to subdue you. In the words of Diana Lamplugh: 'If you hold on to your bag and have the strap round your body you are likely to be dragged along. It is better to keep some money elsewhere on your person and not to fill your bag or briefcase with so many valuable things that you cannot let it go.'

- Even if you have learned self-defence it will only be of limited use if your attacker is bigger and stronger, or if there is more than one person. Learning self-defence may help you to keep your cool, keep your balance and break free to run, but do not assume it will allow you to toss attackers over your shoulder!

- If it comes to a fight try to stay clear of even more dangerous spots than the one you are in; avoid being cornered, steer clear of stairways, roadsides, platform edges at stations, dark areas or objects your attacker could use. It is difficult to remember all this in the heat of the moment, so simply remember to stay in as clear and open an area as possible.

- If you really do have to fight, then go for it! Put every bit of anger and energy into your efforts and fight for your life. Forget about hurting the attacker, just do it and get away. Try to make the first blow count: you may not get another chance.

- If you disable your attacker, get away as fast as you can. Do not stop to see what you have done or to do more. Go straight to where you will find other people, and call the police immediately.

- In fighting back you risk the possibility of a charge of assault. As soon as you can, make notes about what happened – when, where, witnesses, and so on.

- No one can make the decision for you if you are attacked. It is impossible to judge which is the best option. You are either at risk of death or severe injury (in which case you have *no* option) or you can try the other two options first – getting away or attempting to defuse the situation. You will need to keep calm, think clearly, act quickly and decisively, and get away.

Self-defence   Self-defence training was something that many organizations placed great store by in recent years but, more recently still, it has been the focus of much debate. Self-defence has some potential benefits:

- self-protection training has helped many people by increasing their confidence and helping them develop 'automatic' responses, but it still requires regular refresher training as advised by the police;
- by using specific restraint techniques people can be prevented from doing themselves or others harm, given time to calm down, or to get help.

There are a number of important disadvantages, however:

- it can lead to a false sense of security and over-confidence, especially if people do not keep in practice;
- it can lead to people failing to recognize opportunities to calm situations because they are busy planning their defence;
- it is a second best to an outcome where neither party suffers injury;
- much self-defence is very badly taught, and the moves are often unproven, unreliable, and sometimes downright dangerous.

17 Developing assertiveness

When faced with violence it is frequently very difficult to stop reacting long enough to think about and adopt the most appropriate behaviour in response. Often this is because of the shock or surprise, and the emotional and biochemical reactions you are experiencing.

It is possible to learn different ways of behaving and to practise more 'positive' behaviour to a point where you can use it at will, even in difficult situations; one example is assertive behaviour.

Many people have found it helpful because it teaches them about themselves and their own 'usual' or 'habitual' behaviour patterns; it teaches them about a range of behaviour that they may experience from others, and, on a practical level, it teaches strategies for managing interactions with others.

Assertive behaviour

Assertive behaviour describes ways of relating to and interacting with other people that recognize and respect the rights, feelings, needs and opinions of both parties. It is an approach to communicating in which self-respect and respect for other people is demonstrated, and it requires awareness and the taking of responsibility for oneself as well as enabling other people to do the same. Assertiveness is not about getting what you want all the time.

The concept of assertiveness is probably best understood by contrasting assertive behaviour with other types of behaviour, such as aggressive behaviour, manipulative behaviour and behaviour that is variously described as 'passive', 'submissive' or 'non-assertive' – here described as 'passive' (see Table 17.1).

Table 17.1 Some characteristics of aggressive, manipulative and passive behaviour

AGGRESSIVE	MANIPULATIVE	PASSIVE
Recognizing own rights only	Avoiding direct approach	Acting as a 'doormat'
Forceful expressions of opinion	Covert expressions of views	Failure to express views
Need to prove superiority	Skills at deceiving	Decision-making problems
Giving orders rather than requests	Need to be in control	Blaming others
Blaming others	Not trusting self or others	Resignation
Putting people down	Denial of feelings	Giving in
Not listening to others	Insincerity	Saying 'yes'– meaning 'no'
Competitiveness	Making veiled threats	Complaining behind the scenes
Verbal abuse, insults	Using guilt as a weapon	Not knowing own boundaries
Over-reacting	Sabotage behind the scenes	
Egocentricity	Using derogatory language	
Threats	Talking behind people's backs	

Assertive behaviour is characterized by:

- self-respect and self-esteem;
- respect for others;
- recognition of your own and others' rights;
- acceptance of your own positive and negative qualities and those of others;
- acknowledging your own responsibility for your choices and actions;
- recognizing your own needs, wants, and feelings, being able to express them, and allowing others to do the same;
- listening to others;
- being able to ask for your own needs to be met and risk refusal;
- accepting that you do not always get what you want; feeling rejection but not being destroyed by it;
- open and honest interaction with others;
- knowing your own limits; ability to say 'no' and respect others' limits or boundaries;
- giving feedback or constructive criticism when it is due, accepting it of yourself if valid, or rejecting it if it is not.

To sum up: assertive behaviour involves respecting yourself and your own rights while also respecting others and their rights. It requires taking responsibility for yourself and allowing others to do the same for themselves. Assertive behaviour does not guarantee you will always get what you want. It is not about winning and losing, but rather about win–win situations, where both parties are considered and treated as equal and the outcome is acceptable to both – even if one or other party does not get everything they wanted – because the reasons for it are understood.

Assertive behaviour is reflected in the words that are used, but also by the non-verbal communication that accompanies it, for example:

- direct eye contact, but not peering or staring; showing attentiveness and listening;
- relaxed posture, normally well-balanced, not fidgeting;
- facing people, but not threatening – rather, giving them your attention;
- gestures in keeping with what is being said or felt – not agitated or nervous;
- open posture, without arms tightly folded or legs knotted around each other;
- firm, clear tone of voice, but with appropriate expression of feeling.

Assertive behaviour is the most positive of the four approaches – aggressive, manipulative, passive, assertive. Learning assertive behaviour can be helpful in a number of ways, for example:

- When faced with stressful situations, an assertive approach helps you to deal with stress by boosting self-confidence and self-esteem as you consciously acknowledge your rights and needs in a situation.
- Assertiveness can help develop a balanced self-image, acknowledging your worth as a person, your abilities and qualities without becoming arrogant, while being able to recognize and accept faults and mistakes that you can then work on without punishing yourself.
- Assertiveness can help in controlling emotions such as anxiety because you can use learnt behaviour to prevent the emotions getting in the way but without denying them.
- If you feel frustration or anger, assertive approaches will enable the appropriate expression of feelings rather than expressing them aggressively or bottling them up so that they become a problem later.
- Being assertive makes it easier for others to be assertive, because it is a straightforward way of behaving.
- Demonstrating assertive behaviour can provide others with a model of effective behaviour that they can use too.
- Using assertive behaviour in difficult situations can take courage and be stressful in the short term; however, the more you do it the easier it becomes.
- Assertive behaviour avoids you having the 'leftover' feelings associated with other sorts of behaviour – for example, guilt if you are aggressive or manipulative, kicking yourself if you are passive and give in.

Learning to be assertive

A first step in learning to be assertive is to be clear about your rights and those of other people. You have the right:

- to state your needs, ask for what you want;
- to set your own priorities;
- to be treated with respect;
- to express your feelings, opinions and beliefs;
- to say 'yes' or 'no' for yourself;
- to be treated as an equal human being;
- to make mistakes;
- to change your mind;
- to say 'I don't understand';
- to not seek approval;
- to decide for yourself;
- to decide whether or not you are responsible for solving others' problems.

It may seem unnecessary to list the rights people have, but few of us consciously think about our rights at any time, let alone when we are in difficult situations, particularly if they involve aggressive behaviour towards us. For example, it is difficult to refuse to take responsibility for someone's problem when they are blaming you for it or when you are the representative of the organization they believe to have caused the problem.

Similarly, it takes quite an effort to confront a patronizing manager who treats you as an inferior, even though you know you have a right to respect and to be treated as an equal human being.

Rights are not one-sided: just as you have these rights, so does everyone else. As with all rights, these bring with them responsibilities: first, responsibility to ourselves to stand up for our rights, and second, the responsibility to respect the rights of others.

Like all skills, assertiveness needs practice in the appropriate context; from that experience we can go on learning and developing the skills. It is not easy to learn to be assertive or to assert yourself in difficult situations, but once you know the principles you just have to keep practising until it becomes second nature.

The following examples describe the assertive approach to the sort of interactions we all commonly experience at work.

Making requests

- Before you can make requests assertively, it is necessary to know exactly what you want or need.
- In clarifying what it is you want or need you may have to stop thinking about what other people believe you ought to have. Their expectations of you, or your perception of their expectations, can get in the way of you knowing what you want or need.
- This may sound selfish, probably because many of us are socialized out of expressing plainly our wants and needs in favour of what we should do or doing the things that must be done.
- It is often easier to say what we don't want than what we do want. In the workplace one often hears 'Don't bother me with that now', as opposed to 'I want you to hang on to that until this afternoon's meeting and give it to me then.'
- Far from being selfish, clearly expressing your needs and wants helps the listener. It is a straightforward way of communicating that does not leave them guessing.
- If it is easier or more natural to start from the negative, do so. Decide what you don't want, work out the ideal alternative to that and what you will settle for – your fall-back position – if the ideal is not on offer.

- Decide who you need to make the request to: this must be someone who can do something about it. Approaching or complaining to someone not involved or without the power to meet your request is a waste of time but a common feature of working life. One often hears people complaining to peers about their line manager – 'I want him/her to listen to me', or 'I want him/her to tell me how I'm getting on', rather than saying it to the manager.

- When making a request to someone be sure you have their attention first. It is no good plucking up the courage if the other person is only half-listening or doing something else at the same time. Arrange a meeting time formally if you need to do that to ensure the other person's time and attention.

- When you make the request, do so clearly and concisely; say what you want or need positively and specifically; speak for yourself rather than generalizing, and demonstrate appropriate strength of feeling through your tone of voice and body language.

- You don't have to go in with 'both feet' or 'all guns blazing'; that is much more likely to be, or appear, aggressive. Try starting off requests by saying, for example:

  - 'Will you please . . . ?'
  - 'Would you . . . ?'
  - 'Could you please . . . ?'
  - 'I'd like you to . . . '
  - 'I'd prefer you to . . . '

- There is a wide range of possible responses to requests, from agreement to direct refusal; some of them will be more difficult to deal with than others. If you get an unsatisfactory response you will need to decide if your request is important enough to persist with.

- Sticking to your request is one form of persistence, and you should repeat it, perhaps in slightly different but no less clear ways, until it is heard, understood and taken seriously.

- Reflecting the response you get and sticking to your request is another way of persisting, so:

  - pay attention to the other person's response;
  - respond to relevant questions – ignore irrelevant ones that would divert you;
  - summarize what the other person has said very briefly;
  - make your request again.

- If you do persist in your request you must keep your tone of voice and body language relaxed and calm. You don't want the exchange to become aggressive.

- Persistence is fine until it becomes clear that to persist further would mean failing to respect the other person's rights, needs and wants. At this point you may need to accept you cannot have the ideal and try to achieve your previously identified 'fall-back position' as part of a compromise.

Expressing opinions

One of your rights described earlier is the right to hold an opinion and have it heard. When expressing opinions assertively try to remember:

- You may need to create the opportunity to express your opinion by:
  - arranging to meet someone to put your opinion forward;
  - interrupting if the other person does not give you a chance to speak otherwise;
  - writing to someone.

- In expressing yourself you should make a clear, concise statement of your opinion. Speak for yourself; say 'I think', 'I believe', 'in my opinion', 'it seems to me', rather than generalizing or dressing up your opinion as fact.
- Other people also have the right to their opinions and to have them heard, so give others the chance to speak without interrupting, as far as possible; listen to them, do not belittle their views, and respect their right to a different opinion to yours.
- If someone tries to interrupt you continuously you can either ignore it and continue, or say something like 'let me finish . . . ', or 'hold on, I have not finished yet . . . '. When you *have* finished you can then ask them what they were going to say and listen to them.
- There are times when it is best to agree to disagree and leave it at that.
- Finding the common ground is a very positive step towards reaching agreement. Try to identify where you do agree, and work from that positive point.
- Non-verbal communication is just as important as what you say; avoid adopting a posture or tone of voice that could be construed as aggressive, especially when expressing opposing views.

Discussion

Discussion is a feature of many kinds of activities in the workplace. We all know how many meetings we have to attend! Discussion can serve all sorts of purposes, such as generating ideas, making decisions, canvassing opinions, testing out ideas, resolving problems, creating proposals and plans or building relationships. Everyone involved in the discussion should have something to contribute, otherwise they should not be there. Thus it follows that everyone should have an equal opportunity to join in fully.

Discussions are often unbalanced, however; for example, with one or more people doing most of the talking and others doing the listening. This can leave the talkers feeling the listeners are not contributing and are self-ishly keeping ideas and opinions safely to themselves, while the talkers are sharing and taking the risks. The listeners, on the other hand, may well feel they are being taken for granted, not being noticed, or that people are not interested in them or their views.

An assertive approach to discussion, whatever its purpose, can help you as an individual as well as the process of the discussion, thereby making it more effective from everyone's perspective.

The following are suggestions as to how you could take an assertive approach to discussions:

- While you would normally intervene in the conversation at an appropriate point, you may find that if you cannot get a word in you need to create space for yourself by interrupting. If someone is in full flow it may be hard to attract attention away from what they are saying. Try using a phrase that gives the speaker a chance to switch their attention to you and makes it clear you want to contribute, such as:

    - 'I'd like to comment on that . . . '
    - 'I want to make a point here . . . '
    - 'May I just add . . . '
    - 'Before we lose the point . . . '

- If you need to interrupt, use body language as well to demonstrate that there is no aggression on your part – you just want to speak. Appropriate body language can also help defuse any defensive aggression from the person interrupted.
- When you are speaking, do not allow people to interrupt you until you have had a reasonable time to have your say. Stick to your point, say 'let me finish'. Demonstrate by body language, too, that you don't want to take over but just want an equal chance to put your point across.
- Acknowledge that there may be times when you go on too long and other people will interrupt you for that reason; you must respect their right to a say as well.
- Give other people the chance to respond to what you have said.
- If people are not acknowledging what you have said or responding to it, try asking open questions such as 'How do you see it?', 'What do you think?', or 'What were you going to say?'

- In some discussions you may have to persist in breaking into the conversation in order to assert your right to equal opportunity of expression. Most people eventually get the message that you want to take an equal part in the proceedings.
- If people do not get the message that you want to contribute on an equal basis with others, you may have to raise it as a problem. Don't blame people; simply say how you feel and what you want people to do differently.
- Should you find yourself doing most of the talking, you may have to stay deliberately quiet at times and/or invite other people to speak by asking questions or seeking a view from them.
- If you are doing most of the talking it may be that you need to practise listening skills. One way is to listen to the speaker, picking out the key points of what they are saying so that at the end you can summarize what they have said.
- Observe body language so that you know when to stop talking: people fiddling or doodling, slumped in their chairs or gazing out the window may well be indicating that they have listened enough.
- Behaviour in a group can sometimes be unacceptable to some or all of the members – for example, racist or sexist language, mocking someone, swearing or outright aggression towards a group member. An assertive approach to handling such a situation would be:

  - not to accuse or blame;
  - to own the problem and explain: for example, 'I am upset by that sort of language because . . .' or 'I feel really put down when you say . . .', followed by a clear statement of what you want, an assertive request: 'I'd prefer you not to . . .', or 'Would you stop . . .?'

Saying 'No'

Saying 'yes' when you really mean, or want to say, 'no' can leave you feeling exploited or 'put upon'. You may end up resenting other people and getting angry with yourself because you are expending time and energy on others' priorities rather than your own. Responding to everyone else's requests can give you a short-term feeling of being helpful, cooperative and supportive, but you may find you get little job satisfaction from doing others' tasks and have little time to devote to your own job and developing yourself in it.

Eventually the standard of your work may be affected because you take on too much, and that, combined with resentment of yourself and others, can result in depression. Being a martyr can ultimately bring out the worst in the nicest people.

Saying 'no' can be difficult and stressful at the start, but it gets easier with practice and offsets the longer-term risks of not doing so.

Negotiation

Assertiveness is sometimes about refusing requests, saying 'no', and thus not cooperating. It can also mean total cooperation if appropriate; between the two extremes lie negotiation and compromise. Negotiation and compromise are commonly needed in many workplaces in all kinds of circumstances, from sorting out some interpersonal tiff to major management and union negotiations. Assertive negotiation involves:

- deciding on your ideal preference in the situation, and how strongly you feel about achieving it;
- deciding a 'fall-back position' – a second-order preference that you will settle for;
- communicating your ideal preference and the strength of your feeling about it to the other person(s);
- finding out the ideal preference of the other party, and their strength of feeling about it;
- taking into account the preferences and feelings of both sides; deciding if/when it is appropriate to reveal your second preference;
- finding out what the other party is willing to settle for; if you have not done so already, revealing your second preference;
- establishing agreement with the other party if at all possible;
- sticking to your guns about your second preference if the other party tries to push you beyond that;
- being prepared for give and take in the process, but knowing what your boundaries are and communicating them clearly;
- accepting that not every negotiation will achieve the ideal win–win result, where everyone feels that they have achieved something and they agree to and are committed to the outcome.

Feedback

Feedback is a way of giving people information about how they affect us or obtaining information about how we affect others. Skilful feedback is a helpful, enabling, learning process, whether it is critical or complimentary.

Giving and receiving feedback is a form of assertive communication, but it does not always come easily to us. People are often not good at giving or receiving compliments or constructive criticism – partly through a lack of skills and practice, and partly through fear of hurting or embarrassing themselves or others.

When giving feedback, start with the positive. It can help the receiver to hear first what you like, appreciate, enjoy or what you feel they did well. We can easily slip into emphasizing the negative – the focus being on mistakes rather than strengths – and, in the rush to criticize, the positive aspects are overlooked. If the positive is registered first, the negative is more likely to be listened to and acted upon.

Be specific so that you do not leave the listener guessing, and only give feedback on what can be changed. Giving feedback to someone about something over which they have little or no control or choice is not only unhelpful, it is pointless, and can create frustration and resentment.

Timing is important. Feedback is often most useful as early as possible after the event, so that behaviour and feelings are remembered accurately. However, it is important to be as sure as possible that the receiver is ready for the feedback at that stage; in some situations it may be more helpful to reserve feedback until later.

In situations where you offer negative feedback, suggesting what could have been done differently is often more helpful than simply criticizing. Turn the negative feedback into a positive suggestion, such as 'I know everyone was eager to get on with the business when I brought the new manager in today, but you did seem unwelcoming; perhaps next time we can stop for a moment to introduce everyone properly.'

Don't assume the feedback you give is immediately understood, or that the message received was the message intended. Check with the other person to ensure understanding.

Feedback which demands change or tries to impose it on the receiver invites resistance and may lead to aggression. Feedback is not about telling people what they must do, but what is preferable from the giver's point of view.

Try to be objective. Offering facts before opinions and describing observable behaviour helps to avoid total subjectivity. It can also help put observations into context and give the listener information about the behaviour, as well as its effects on you from your perspective.

Giving critical feedback

- Even well-intended, constructive criticism won't necessarily make you popular; you need to decide what is important: being liked or getting the message across.
- If criticism is due, it may be kinder to make it sooner rather than later, thus offering the receiver the chance to do something about it now – criticism should be given in private, preferably face-to-face, and make sure there is enough time to discuss it.
- Be clear about what you prefer the listener to do. Make sure the listener understands the positive and negative consequences of acting or not

acting on the criticism.
- If you are uncomfortable or awkward about criticizing you can say so – for example, 'It's difficult for me to say this, but I think you should know . . . ', or 'I'm concerned about upsetting you but I feel I must tell you . . . because . . . '
- You may need to persist with the feedback if you meet resistance and you really feel it is essential to get the point over.
- End on a positive note: thank the receiver for listening, and set the criticism in the context of what they do well.

Giving complimentary feedback   Expressions of appreciation would help the atmosphere of many workplaces. When giving a compliment, make sure that it is genuine, and not made for other ends.

Receiving feedback   Feedback can be uncomfortable to hear sometimes, but it is better than not knowing what others think and feel. Listen to the feedback because it may help you; you will remain entitled to ignore it if you decide it is irrelevant, insignificant or about behaviour you wish to maintain for other reasons.

Make sure you understand what the giver of feedback is saying before you respond. Avoid jumping to conclusions, becoming defensive or going on the attack, as all these will deter people from giving you feedback. Check you have understood by asking questions or by paraphrasing what you believe was said.

If you rely on only one source of information, you may get a very individual or biased view. Ask other people for feedback, as you may find they experience you differently. The more information you have, the more likely you are to develop a balanced view of yourself and keep feedback in perspective.

Receiving complimentary feedback   Accepting compliments can be difficult but, like gifts, if they are not accepted the giver may feel hurt, rejected or humiliated and is unlikely to try to give again. Compliments should be accepted without embarrassment. It sometimes takes practice to simply say 'Thank you', or 'It is kind of you to say so', or 'It's nice to be appreciated.' You can always say 'I'm a little embarrassed but thank you': that way people know why you are reacting as you are, but that you do not want them to avoid complimenting you.

If you believe the giver of the compliment has an ulterior motive, accept the compliment and deal with the hidden agenda at a separate time.

Receiving critical feedback   Constructive, well-timed and supportive criticism can still be very uncomfortable to receive, especially if you have been on the receiving end of damaging criticism in the past. On the other hand it can be very beneficial.

There is nothing worse than discovering too late you could have done something better or differently (the 'I wish I'd known' syndrome). Accept valid criticism without being defensive, justifying yourself, making excuses or passing the buck.

If you do not accept the criticism, you can reject it without rejecting the other person: say you 'disagree', but not 'You are wrong.' The latter is a confrontational response, inviting the other person to prove the opposite.

If the giver of criticism makes generalizations such as 'You always do . . . ', you can find out exactly what they are getting at by explaining you are unclear and asking questions, for example, 'What exactly did I do or say . . . ?', 'Can you give me an example of . . . ?', 'Can you describe what it is that . . . ?' In this way you can pinpoint your behaviour that gave rise to the criticism and help identify the emotional effects of your actions on others. If you explain that you need more information and ask questions in a way that is not defensive, challenging or aggressive, you can obtain the necessary information to decide whether or not you agree with the criticism.

Another aspect of questions is that they can help demonstrate when criticism is unfair or vindictive, because the giver is unlikely to be able to provide the information, examples, descriptions and so on to support the criticism. In view of this you can clearly state that you disagree; the process may put the person off future unfair or vindictive criticism.

When the criticism is intended to be, or proves to be, helpful to you, always thank the giver; it may have been difficult for them to give, and constructive criticism is a practice that should be encouraged.

18 Travel guidelines

Health care involves travel to the usual place of work; to other organizations; to visit patients at home or in hostels, hospitals or prison, and to attend meetings in a variety of settings. It may also involve overnight stays in hotels. These guidelines are designed to help the individual worker to take sensible precautions to protect personal safety when away from the usual place of work.

Travelling on foot

Travelling on foot is often the easiest and quickest way of getting around, especially in a town or city. It is generally a safe means of travel, but the risks increase, of course, when it is dark, as it is on winter afternoons.

The following guidelines provide advice on keeping safe on foot:

- Think ahead, be alert and aware of your surroundings.
- Try to avoid walking alone at night.
- Keep to busy, well-lit roads.
- Do not take short cuts.
- Avoid poorly-lit or quiet underpasses.
- Walk facing oncoming traffic to avoid kerb crawlers.
- If you have to walk in the same direction as the traffic and a driver stops, simply turn and walk the other way; the driver cannot follow immediately.
- If a driver stops, write down the registration number; the driver will almost certainly leave immediately.

Public transport

'Public transport' here includes buses, trains and underground services.

- Always sit near the bus driver on a driver-only bus, or stay downstairs on a double-decker bus with a conductor.
- If possible, wait for the bus at a busy stop that is well-lit, or a bus stop close to areas of activity – for example, a garage or a late shop.
- Have your fare ready in your hand or pocket, separate from other money or valuables.
- Try to avoid having your hands full with heavy bags.
- Wear sensible shoes in case you need to move fast; be ready to kick off other shoes if necessary.
- On trains, single enclosed compartments are now fairly rare, but when you see them, avoid them. Sit in an open compartment near the alarm pull if you can, or at least register where it is.
- If there is a guard on the train sit in the nearest compartment to the guard's van.
- In stations, note where the exits are so you can leave readily.
- Don't doze off: stay alert to what is going on around you.
- If you do not like the look of someone, change carriages.
- In underground stations, keep your eyes open and note the exits and station alarm panel.
- On tube trains, sit in busy compartments.
- Carry a personal alarm in your hand – it is no use in a bag.
- Avoid travelling alone late at night on any form of public transport if at all possible.

Using cabs

In London, Hackney carriages (black taxis) are licensed by the police. Each cab carries white plates with black lettering, giving the licence number, both inside the cab and on the outside. The driver must wear a badge in a conspicuous place. In London these are always 'black cabs'. At the moment (1994) mini-cabs are unlicensed in London. However, this is under review, and the Select Committee on Transport has recommended tight regulation for mini-cabs and their drivers. Most mini-cab drivers are reliable and honest, but like all occupations, they have their exceptions. Outside London fairly rigorous checks are already in place.

- Make sure you have the 'phone number of a reputable cab

company. Your employing agency may well have a contract with a local taxi firm.

- When you book your cab, ask the company for the driver's name and call sign. Ask what type of car is being used.
- If you are telephoning from a public place, try to avoid doing so where someone can overhear you giving your name and so on. Anyone could pull up and call 'Cab for Mary Smith', so when your cab arrives, check the driver's name and confirm the company's name.
- If you can, share a cab with a friend.
- Whilst you may not wish to appear unfriendly, always sit in the back.
- If you do chat with the driver, don't give any personal details away.
- If you feel uneasy with the driver, ask to stop at a busy, familiar place and get out.
- Have your cash ready before you arrive at your destination; then leave the cab and pay the driver.
- Have your door keys ready and enter your home quickly.

Beware of bogus mini-cabs! Some people do not work for mini-cab firms at all, but put an aerial on the roof of their car and have an imitation handset. They unlawfully ply for hire at busy night spots, and gain fares by calling out 'Someone ordered a cab?' On a busy night with a shortage of transport it could be tempting, but it is much safer to wait.

Using private cars

During recent years a number of incidents have occurred in which individuals have been attacked while using their private cars. Most of these have been thefts, mainly of mobile 'phones and money – and sometimes of cars. The following guidelines are designed to help individuals develop their own personal safety strategy for using their own cars, whether in the course of their work or for leisure purposes.

Whether the car you are using is your own vehicle, leased through your employer, or hired or provided by your employing agency, the following guidelines apply:

- Keep your car in good working order, have it serviced regularly, and check it regularly yourself.
- If you hire a car, ensure it has been checked or check it yourself.
- Carry extra petrol in a safety-approved portable petrol can.
- Join one of the breakdown/rescue organizations; employers often pay for this if you are required to use your car on business, or it is usually part of the package when you lease a car or have a company car.

- Consider a car 'phone if you travel a lot; in some cases an employer may provide one or contribute towards the cost of it. Car 'phones/mobile 'phones are excellent confidence-boosters, but remember that they are also a high theft risk so do keep them out of sight. They are an invaluable help in planning and in letting people know where you are and how you are getting to your destination. In an emergency the 'phone will not indicate your whereabouts, however, so it is vital to keep alert and to know where you are – this means watching out for signs and taking note of your surroundings.
- Make sure you have change and a 'phone card for use in an emergency.
- Plan your route, know where you are going and how to get there.
- Always have the necessary maps and directions in the car so you do not have to stop to ask.
- Tell someone where you are going. If you change your mind, let someone know.
- Stay in the car as much as possible. Keep the doors locked and windows closed when you can, especially in towns when you must stop at lights, junctions, and so on.
- Keep handbags, briefcases, medical bags and so on out of reach of open windows in case of snatch thieves. 'Car jackers' work in groups of three or four. One looks for a car driven by a person on their own and which has a saleable object such as a portable telephone, bag or briefcase on the seat; they signal to a second member of the gang, who diverts the driver by, for example, the sale of flowers or windscreen washing; the third gang member opens the car door (if it is unlocked) or breaks the window, snatches the item and quickly disappears!
- When leaving the car, always lock medical bags, equipment, luggage, valuables and so on in the boot. Leave nothing on display.
- Lock your car, even if you only go to pay for petrol on a garage forecourt.
- When you park in daylight, consider what the area will be like in the dark.
- At night, park in a well-lit place, and one that is busy, if possible. Avoid multi-storey car parks or car parks where you and your vehicle are not clearly visible. Choose AA/Police Gold or Silver Star car parks – they are much the safest.
- Before you get in the car check the back seat: carry a torch on your person for this purpose.
- If you see an incident or accident, or someone tries to flag you down, don't stop to investigate. Is it safe? Could you help? Would it be safer and more use if you went for help? If a police officer signals you to stop always ask for their identity card before opening the window. You

need not get out of your car on a motorway: instead, you can signal the police officer or car that you will lead them to a garage or police station. This also applies to unmarked police cars and to plain-clothes police.

- If a car pulls up in front of you and you have to stop, keep the engine running; if you turn if off and then try to restart it in a hurry you may flood the carburettor.
- If you think you are being followed, try to alert other drivers – use the lights and horn. Keep driving until you reach a busy area, a police, fire or ambulance station, or a garage. Keep a distance between you and the car in front.
- If anyone approaches you in your car when you are stationary, stay in the car with the doors locked and the windows closed. If the engine is running, keep it running; if not, start the car. If you are in any doubt at all, drive off; if you can't, make as much noise and fuss as possible.
- Any attempt to force entry into your car, such as someone trying to force down a partially open window, may need to be met with force. Use your personal alarm if it is to hand, but also consider using de-icer spray, the heel of your shoe, or the cigar lighter. If you can surprise the attacker the advantage is yours and you can get away.
- Avoid taking people (patients or other contacts) in your car on your own unless they are friends or very well-known to you.

Motorways

Travel on motorways is a cause for concern, especially when a breakdown occurs or assistance is needed. Opinions are divided as to what is best to do, so use your judgement according to the circumstances:

- If you can drive safely to an emergency telephone then do so, stopping with the front passenger door of the car level with the telephone, and as close to it as possible.
- Switch on your hazard lights; if leaving the vehicle, do so by the near-side door. Leave any animals in the car.
- Never cross the carriageway to reach a closer telephone, and never reverse your car to a telephone.
- If you cannot drive further, a marker post (every 100 metres) will point to the nearest 'phone. 'Phones are set 1 000 metres apart, so you will never need to walk further than 500 metres. No money is required: as soon as you lift the handset it will start ringing in the police control room. You do not need to say where you are; they will know.
- Stand behind the 'phone, facing oncoming traffic, so you can see if anyone approaches you. The passing traffic makes it very noisy so you

may have to shout.
- Tell the control if you are a woman on your own. They will covertly alert a police car to check you are all right if at all possible. On some urban motorways they may be able to see you on closed circuit television.
- If your car is not near the 'phone then note the numbers on the nearest marker post. Tell the control room the problem, and have your breakdown organization card and your registration number ready.

Stay in your car or stand on the verge?   Section 173 of the *Highway Code* advises you to decide whether or not to stay in the car or leave it and stand on the verge. However, 10 per cent of all fatal motorway accidents take place when a vehicle collides with a stationary car parked on the hard shoulder. In 1988, 25 such fatal accidents occurred in this way.

If you are alone and decide to stay in the vehicle, whether you have 'phoned the police first or not, sit in the nearside seat: it gives the impression that there is someone with you nearby. Keep all doors locked and windows closed. If you decide to stay in the car, remember that it could be involved in an accident.

If you decide to stand on the verge, try to stay out of sight of passing cars. Lock all car doors, but leave the passenger door fully open so that you can get back in quickly if you decide to. Then lock the passenger door behind you. Do not leave the keys in the car.

If you are by the 'phone and someone stops, use the 'phone to tell the police and give them the registration number of the car that has stopped. Look at the driver and give a description as you do so.

When the breakdown truck arrives, check that the driver knows your name and has in fact been sent to you. Some breakdown vehicles cruise, waiting to pirate custom. Crime prevention advantages must be weighed against remaining in a vehicle in a potentially hostile environment.

The advice from the Department of Transport, police, RAC and AA is to stay on the verge, only re-entering the car if you feel in danger; try to decide by taking all the factors into consideration: the weather (fog, rain, snow, sunshine), the time of day, and whether it is a dark, deserted country stretch or a busy, well-lit urban area.

Staying in hotels

- Park nearby, if possible, in a well-lit area where you and your vehicle can easily be seen.
- At reception, avoid other people overhearing your name and room number.

- Avoid rooms that are accessible from outside – for example, on the ground floor, or with a fire escape outside.
- If there is a safety chain on the door, or a lock preventing access with a pass key, use it.
- Use a door alarm if you have one.
- Never go to other people's rooms unless you are absolutely sure you are safe.
- Never invite people to your room unless you know you are safe.
- If you hear any disturbance, stay in your room and call for help.
- Do not wander around hotel grounds after dark.
- If you feel safer avoiding the dining room, order your meal in your room.

Part 3

Training for safety

This section provides general guidance for trainers, and a number of sample training programmes, or 'tasks'. These can be used as they stand, or be modified to meet the training needs of particular organizations and groups. In using them, the trainer will be able to draw on the text of Parts 1 and 2 of Personal Safety for Health Care Workers.

Guidelines for trainers

The effectiveness of a personal safety policy will depend on a number of related issues. The organization, and individual employees, will need to be committed to the policy and to the procedures which have been agreed to make the policy work. They will also need training for their role in improving safety levels for themselves and for their colleagues. Training for front-line staff and for their line managers is an essential ingredient in the development of a successful personal safety policy.

When organizations, and trainers within them, embark on training programmes it is not uncommon to discover that the roles of different people in ensuring that the training is effective have been assumed rather than defined. At worst there can be great confusion about who is responsible for what, so that learners, full of enthusiasm and expectations, find themselves unable to apply their learning because the support, organizational changes, finance and so forth are not in place. Investing some time in ensuring there is clarity about, and agreement on, the role of different people in the organization will certainly bear dividends.

If, for example, policy-makers and managers are unprepared to accept their role in financing the changes necessary to ensure safe working, there is little point in raising expectations through training. Similarly, supervisors must be willing to support the development and maintenance of safer working practices if training is to prove effective. Clarity about the roles of various people in ensuring safe working is an essential precursor to gaining their commitment, which is itself essential if the training is to achieve its aim.

It is important to be clear about what is, and what is not, the trainer's role and responsibility, and what can reasonably be expected of him/her. It may be helpful to consider the following areas in determining the role of the trainer, in negotiating that role with others, or in communicating that role to others.

The trainer can reasonably be expected to take responsibility for planning, designing, implementing and evaluating the training. He or she cannot, however, be responsible for policy development or financial decisions, or for solving the organization's or other people's problems.

From the outset the trainer should ensure that managers and policy-makers support the training and are prepared to provide the necessary resources and organizational support to ensure that training is part of an integrated approach to personal safety. A senior manager should work with the trainer to negotiate with personnel, for example, on the implementation of outcomes from training. Training outcomes will also help to inform developing policy and practice, and again a route into the policy-making machinery will be needed. While safety issues should be addressed at all levels within the organization, it is helpful for a senior manager to have a special responsibility for seeing that safety is considered and reviewed on a regular basis, particularly when new services and facilities are being planned.

Values and beliefs

Whether we recognize it consciously or not, all of us operate from a basis of our values and beliefs, and this influences our role as trainers. Our own values and beliefs, as well as those underlying the materials and resources we use, will have an impact on the training and the learners.

Some organizations have their own trainers, but many will buy in personal safety training from independent trainers. When doing so, they will need to be assured of the competence of the trainer, and also of the values and beliefs within which they work. If the organization concerned is within the voluntary sector, for example, the trainer will need to be aware of the value system of that particular agency, and of its special interests and role.

The values and beliefs identified below in respect of safety at work and training people are those which underlie this book. They influence its content, style and expectations of how it should be used by health care workers, managers and trainers.

- Working towards safety is 'our' problem, in the sense that everyone has a responsibility. It should never be a 'them and us' situation, where management are in confrontation with the workforce or unions. To achieve a safe working environment, everyone must play their part.
- People have a right to be safe at work, and managers have a duty in law to ensure they are, as far as possible, safe. Equally, managers have a right to expect support and cooperation, and the workforce has a

responsibility to fulfil these expectations.

- Trainers train and learners learn. No matter how good the trainer, he/she cannot learn for people but can only facilitate their learning. Thus participants have a responsibility to play their part in the learning process.
- Training is most effective when it is learner-centred – that is, the learner's needs, level of experience, preferred style of learning, existing knowledge and working context are all taken into account in designing and providing the training.
- Trainers are enablers of learning – they are a resource, people with expertise and experience (not necessarily expert on content) in designing and providing learning opportunities.
- Training should be safe for people, especially those who come to training events carrying with them images of school, or who are fearful of being challenged, questioned or showing themselves up. Even otherwise confident people can find the new or unusual setting of a training event disconcerting or even threatening. This is particularly important where the content of the training, as in this case, may evoke emotional responses. Trainers have a role in ensuring the training environment is safe by being clear about its purpose, ground rules and norms of behaviour. It also means trainers may need to support individual learners in difficulty, or deal with any inappropriate behaviour.
- Equality is a fundamental consideration throughout training; it should be taken into account in all aspects of the process, for example:

  - a range of food to meet all dietary requirements;
  - accessibility for people with disabilities;
  - services such as brailling or induction loops;
  - resources that are free of racist or sexist language;
  - resources that present positive rather than stereotypical images;
  - timing of training so as to take account of the care responsibilities of the group;
  - provision of a crèche or child care;
  - dates that do not clash with religious or other festivals, or school holidays;
  - language used should not promote stereotypes, for example, habitually referring to a manager as 'he';
  - not making assumptions about people but checking how they wish to be referred to – for example, 'women' or 'ladies'; 'black people' or 'Asian people';
  - staff in a training venue should know what behaviour is expected of them;
  - the venue should be safe – that is, have safe, well-lit car parks, be

secure at night if people are staying, and have transport to and from it if needed;

- everyone should have the opportunity to express views and opinions, and these should be respected.

- Recognizing and using the experience of the learners is important because it:

  - involves them actively in the learning;
  - recognizes the value of their experience and builds on it;
  - can increase the perceived relevance of training to individuals;
  - enables learning from each other in the group, thus helping group development;
  - is generally what people learn most from, so discussion of such experience should be planned.

- Training should be constructive, not destructive. The training should not become an opportunity to criticize or a griping session; this may well be cathartic for the group but is unlikely to help in gaining their commitment to change or recognition of their responsibilities within the process.

- In the context of this training about violence it is important to stress that it is not personal but work-related. The training, while being sensitive to people's experience and feelings, is not a counselling activity but is about the work setting and the development of safe working practices.

Adult learners

As well as having gone through the education system and been at work, adult learners will have considerable life experience. They will have their own values and beliefs; they will have formed their own views and opinions; they will have aspirations and expectations of life and work; they will have their own different motivations for doing things and, generally, have a sense of their individuality and individual needs.

When it comes to training, adults often feel their learning ability is not what it was. Sometimes they have unpleasant memories of school or other training; they may fear loss of status or embarrassment if they cannot immediately cope or compete in the learning situation, and are often apprehensive of a new situation and new people. They will also want to be sure of the relevance of the training and that it is worth giving time to.

Research demonstrates that the rate of learning in some adults may decline with age, just as memory generally reduces in efficiency as we get older, but experience and motivation, combined with well-designed training, can compensate for this.

Bearing all these things in mind, the following points may help in designing and providing training for adult learners:

- Adults will feel more secure if they know where they are being led and how. The aims and objectives of the training should be explained – the role of the trainer as enabler and supporter of learning, and their responsibility as the learners to do the learning – but in a setting that will ensure this is as safe and unthreatening as possible.
- The participants' experience should be acknowledged, and ways designed for them to contribute different ideas, views, opinions and suggestions constructively rather than taking an adversary stance and arguing. This requires time in the programme, which must be planned for.
- It should be established at the start that it is quite normal to feel strange and apprehensive; just knowing that someone else feels the same way can help. Our ability to learn is impaired when emotions such as distress or fear get in the way. It is important that trainers recognize the signs of such emotions and deal with them rather than ignore them.
- An introductory exercise that helps people to share their concerns about the training itself is a good way of relieving tension.
- An effort should be made to establish group norms so that differences are respected and people feel able to express their views, feelings and so on.
- Competitiveness should be kept to a minimum. Activities that require cooperation rather than competition will help.
- Encouragement and the experience of the group should be used to boost confidence – but without a patronizing approach.
- Training should be designed to move from the concrete to the abstract, from the easy to the difficult. Going step by step, learning one thing and building on it, allows people to achieve and grow in confidence. It is also much easier to learn, since few of us can launch into a new subject at the abstract level.
- We all learn and remember through our senses. Research into learning and memory shows that we remember:

  - 10 per cent of what we hear;
  - 50 per cent of what we hear and see;
  - 90 per cent of what we hear, see and do.

  Given this, training designed to stimulate or utilize more than one of the senses at the same time is more likely to be effective in terms of people's learning and retention.
- Remembering is also aided by reinforcing what has been learnt with

reviews, revision, summaries and plenty of practice.
- Trainers should not be surprised if adults don't accept what they say, argue with them, want to change the programme, or raise unexpected issues. They should try to be as flexible as possible, meeting individuals' needs but balancing this with meeting the needs of the rest of the group, and achieving the aims and objectives of the training.
- Training activities should be linked with what people are learning and to the work context. This helps to demonstrate relevance and usefulness in a practical way, and encourages learning.

Identifying training needs

Most trainers will recognize the classic definition of a training need as the gap that exists between the current skills, knowledge, experience, performance, attitudes or behaviour and what is required or desired to do the job now, or in the future, in the organization.

Identifying training needs in relation to safety at work is similar to identifying other needs, in that they may:

- be general organization-wide needs as a result of policy or practice;
- be needs specific to a group of staff who have particular roles or tasks;
- arise as a result of statutory requirements;
- result from previous problems that demonstrate a need for training;
- have been identified by individuals themselves, supervisors or managers;
- result from the observation of, research into, or learning about good practice elsewhere.

It is especially important when identifying needs in this area to be sure that the participants themselves share the trainer's perception of the need. Their commitment to learning and implementing what they learn will be necessary, and will only be forthcoming if they perceive a need for it, its relevance to their work, and its benefits to them as individuals.

In order to achieve this the trainer should consider involving the learners as much as possible in defining their own needs and taking time to ensure that, where needs are 'imposed' – for example, because of statutory or policy requirements – the participants know why these requirements exist and how they are relevant to them.

Aims and learning objectives

An aim is an overall statement of the purpose of the training; it describes in broad terms the intentions of the trainer in providing the training. For example, 'The aim of the training event is to introduce participants to the safety policy and their role in implementing it', or 'The training course is designed to ensure all reception staff can operate the new security procedures.'

A learning objective is a much more detailed statement of what will be learned by individuals if the training is completely successful. There are five principles in writing learning objectives:

1 They should always be written with the focus on the learner.
2 They involve making statements about observable behaviour.
3 They define the specific area in which learning will be applied.
4 They should state the acceptable standard of performance.
5 They should state the conditions under which the new behaviour can be displayed.

Simply, this means that learning objectives state what the learner will be able to do, to what standard, and under what conditions. For example, the numbers in what follows show how each of the principles is incorporated in the learning objective:

> 'The reception staff (1) will be able to demonstrate each step (2) in the front desk security procedure (3) fully and correctly (4) without assistance from a supervisor (5).'

Drawing up learning objectives is not always easy, especially where what is being learnt is not readily measurable or assessable. The process is easier if expressions like 'know', 'appreciate', 'comprehend', 'be familiar with', 'realize' or 'understand' are avoided. These describe things that are far from observable (principle 2). It is not possible to see a person 'appreciate' something, or assess to what extent they 'realize' something, unless they act or behave in a way that demonstrates this.

More useful expressions include 'state', 'describe', 'explain', 'demonstrate', 'identify', 'list', 'prioritize', 'solve', 'perform' and 'operate', because these words specify actions that can be seen and assessed.

Drawing up aims and objectives for training and learning may seem time-consuming, but it is very useful because:

● it helps the trainer to clarify the purpose of the training and the outcomes in terms of what the learners will learn;

- the discipline of writing them down, even if it takes time at the beginning, saves time later in identifying appropriate resources and activities;
- they provide a basis for evaluation, something against which to measure success;
- clear aims and objectives make communication about the training much easier, whether the trainer is involved in 'selling' the idea to policy-makers and managers, or using them to 'market' the training to potential learners;
- aims and objectives not only show the 'destination' of the training but map out the 'route' to be taken to get there.

This can ensure that the trainer and the learners have clarity about the process and confidence in it.

Motivating learners

If people are motivated to learn, they are much more likely to learn more readily, perform well and enjoy the process of learning. Generally people are motivated to learn if they are interested, curious, can see personal progress, achievement, reward or added responsibility as a result of learning.

If the design and implementation of training attracts and holds attention, arouses interest and curiosity, and is relevant to the learners in terms of the personal benefits they perceive it will have for them, this will have helped to motivate them. Aspects to consider when designing training include the following:

- **Realism** – making the learning experience real: participants need to see, do, feel, hear as much as possible in the process.
- **Curiosity** – learning should be designed as a puzzle or a problem-solving process, and participants encouraged to seek solutions.
- **Variety** – beware of boredom! Varying methods and aids will encourage participation and activity.
- **Incentives** – people should understand why they are learning something, and be aware of its relevance and benefit to them, their job and their future.
- **Achievement** – progress made should be stressed, and opportunities provided for participants to demonstrate new-found skills and knowledge.
- **Environment** – the environment should be as pleasant and relaxed as possible, and people's needs for comfort met (fresh air, warmth, drinks, meals and so on). Interruptions and distractions should be

avoided.

- **Enthusiasm** – the trainer must be enthusiastic and interested or the learners will not be!
- **Involvement** – wherever possible, the learners should be involved in the process of deciding about the design, content and running of the training. Nothing motivates people more than being clear about what they need and want, and having confidence that participation in a particular activity will provide it.

Planning training

Planning a training event, like planning anything, usually involves making judgements and decisions while taking into account all sorts of complex and interlinked factors. This process can be simplified by posing some basic questions at the outset, to guide the planner through planning and to avoid missing aspects out. The following checklists, although not exhaustive, pose some key questions in planning:

- **What**

    - are the needs that have been identified?
    - is the training intended to achieve: its aims and objectives?
    - is the event: a two-hour session, a week's course?
    - can realistically be achieved in the time?
    - approach is best and is possible in the time?
    - resources are required (people, funds, equipment, materials)?
    - is the trainer good at, confident doing?
    - help is needed (administrative, specialist input)?

- **Who**

    - is the training for (adults, particular group of staff, cross-section of staff)?
    - is responsible for what (for example, bookings, printing materials, briefing people, presenting, evaluation)?
    - need to be communicated with: for example, co-trainers or contributors to do the planning, participants about arrangements, managers about outcomes of training?
    - is responsible for follow-up action?
    - should be involved in decisions about the training: managers, participants, trainers?
    - are the trainers? Why have they been chosen? What is their particular expertise and experience?

- **When**
    - will the training take place? If it is part of a series, does it need to fit in with other things? Will the timing exclude people: for example, parents in school holidays, part-time staff? Does the timing allow for planning, preparation, briefing and so on? Can others involved meet the timescale?
    - do people need to have information about the training and their part in it? Has their commitment been obtained and necessary bookings made?

- **Where**
    - will the event take place? Is there a choice about where it is held? Will it be in the workplace or outside – which is preferable and why? (bear in mind interruptions and whether people are contactable). Does the venue meet equal opportunities criteria in terms of access and services? Is the environment appropriate: space, heating, light, comfortable seats, noise, training equipment and facilities?
    - are people travelling from? Is there public transport that can be safely used? Are there parking facilities that are safe?

- **How**
    - will the effectiveness of the training be evaluated and how will these data inform future training and practice?
    - will the training be followed up: for example, by further training, supporting learners, organizational changes?
    - will the trainer manage difficult people in a group, potentially contentious issues, conflict, a situation where someone gets upset or needs particular help, the group saying 'This is not what we want', demands for management to change practices?

- **Why**
    - is the training being planned? The trainer should ensure that there is support for it in the organization and that there are not unreasonable expectations that the training itself will solve all the problems or automatically bring about change.

Once these issues have been addressed a training programme can be produced. It is likely to include some or all of the following:

- **Aim** – a general statement of the purpose of the training.
- **Objectives** – specific statements describing what the participants will learn and be able to do as a result.

- **Target group** – who the training is for, why they need it, how they will benefit, and how it links to their work or other training.
- **Timing** – when it will take place: dates and times; all the times of a series of events should be shown.
- **Location** – where the training will take place: facilities and limitations of the venue, for example access; how to get there; where the rooms to be used are.
- **The trainer(s)** – who will do the training: internal trainers or outside specialists. Their names and perhaps some information about them, such as background and experience, should be given.
- **Content** – information about the content of the training.
- **Approach** – a description of the approach to be taken in the training event. This could include a statement such as: 'The approach will be varied, involving input by trainers and participative activities.'
- **Evaluation** – how the effectiveness of the training will be assessed and when, for example:

  - by a questionnaire at the end of the event;
  - by peer or self-assessment during training;
  - by assessment back in the workplace.

- **Contacts** – the training co-ordinator's name and how to contact them, and also how to contact the venue.

Evaluating training

Evaluation processes are generally used to obtain information about the results of training. This information is then used to assess the value and effectiveness of the training with a view to improving it if necessary. This is an important part of the training process because evaluation helps to demonstrate whether the aims and objectives of the training have been achieved. Effectiveness can be shown where training has resulted in changed behaviour or practice, or changes in the quality of service. Ways in which training can be developed or made more effective can emerge, as can problems, difficulties or further training needs.

The appropriateness of training for particular groups of staff, or for people undertaking particular roles or tasks, can be assessed. Evaluation can also highlight the absence of, or uneconomical use of, resources such as money, time, space, materials or personnel. It provides useful feedback to those who were involved at any stage – for example, by backing the decision to embark on the training – and to those who provided the training, as well as to the participants themselves.

Evaluating training is much easier where clear aims and objectives have been set in the first place. There are many ways of obtaining information for evaluation purposes:

- a questionnaire can be used at the end of a session, event or programme to obtain immediate reactions;
- a questionnaire can be used some weeks or months after the training to help assess if learning has been remembered and/or used in the workplace;
- an exercise can be designed for during or after the training to collect information – for example, participants can be invited to write comments under appropriate headings on pieces of flipchart paper pinned around the room – this is called the 'graffiti exercise';
- learners can be asked to comment verbally at the end of the training on its value, and their responses recorded;
- learners can be visited at the workplace some time after the training and interviewed to obtain comments;
- discussion with the participants' line managers after the event can gather their views on how the learner has developed;
- participants can be asked to record their views at a later stage, and their comments compared with their views immediately after the event;
- the group can be brought together again for an evaluation session, and asked to comment on the particular aspects about which information is needed;
- participants can be asked to keep a diary for an agreed time after the training, and record if, when and how they used the learning.

These are just a few ideas for collecting evaluation data. There are many other methods – some very complex – that can be used, but the most important thing to remember is that there is no point in evaluating unless those responsible for training provision are prepared to take note of the findings and make any necessary changes, even if this means admitting mistakes, poor decisions or performance, and errors of judgement.

Task 1 Introduction to violence at work

Aim

To increase awareness of the problem of violence at work and how to keep safe.

Objectives

At the end of the programme the participants will be able to:

- say what is meant by violence at work;
- identify risks they may face at work;
- describe actions they will take to ensure safety at work.

Time

Two-and-a-half hours.

Target groups

All staff who need an introduction to the subject of violence at work and keeping safe. This programme could also be included in a general health and safety programme.

171

Resources

Flipcharts and stand, pens, any prepared materials or handouts.

Environment

A room large enough for the whole group to sit comfortably in a circle and for people to split up to work in pairs for a short time.

Timetable

1	Introduction	15 mins
2	What do we mean by violence at work?	30 mins
3	Minimizing risk	1 hour
4	Safer practice – personal action plan	30 mins
5	Summary/evaluation	15 mins

Contents

1 Introduction

- Introduce yourself and the training programme, saying what the aims and objectives are.
- Ask the group members to introduce themselves.
- Give any 'housekeeping' information, such as time you will finish, location of facilities, and so on.

2 What do we mean by violence at work?

- Gather the group's ideas of what violence at work is.
- Discuss what they would include in the term 'violence at work' and what they would exclude, and why.
- Explain to, or show the group, how other people define violence at work (see Handout 1).
- Ensure the group understands violence is used as an all-embracing term to cover a range of behaviour and its effects.

3   Minimizing risk

- Identify areas of work you know the group is involved in or familiar with – for example, reception, travelling, dealing with the public, handling money. Go through each area asking the group to identify risks or potential risks, adding to their ideas if necessary. Record their ideas on a flipchart.
- Go back through each of the areas and the risks identified in it, asking the group to suggest actions that could be taken to reduce the risk or to avoid it altogether. Add to the group's suggestions if necessary.
- Decide with the group members which of the actions they have identified can be taken by them individually or as a group, and which need management agreement and support or the support of others. Record this.

4   Safer practice – personal action plan

- Individuals prepare a personal action plan, listing actions they can take independently to minimize the risks they face, and any actions they can take to bring risks that need action from others to the attention of the appropriate people.
- As the group members complete action plans, ask them to look through them again and put deadlines on their actions where possible; this will encourage them to stick to their decisions.

5   Summary/evaluation

- Summary: go back over the key learning points:
  - what we mean by violence at work;
  - areas of risk identified;
  - ideas for minimizing risks;
  - actions people have decided to take.

- Evaluation: either:
  - conduct a brief evaluation on the content and conduct of the programme, venue and so on, or
  - explain how the programme will be evaluated later.

Task 2 The manager's role

Aim

To ensure managers are aware of their duties and roles in ensuring the safety of employees at work.

Objectives

At the end of the programme participants will be able to:

- explain their duties as employers in respect of employee safety;
- identify why action in the workplace on safety is necessary;
- prepare an action plan for themselves to assist in developing safety measures.

Time

Three-and-a-half hours.

Target groups

Managers, specifically those whose roles involve them in policy development and implementation and who have had no prior training in managing violence at work.

Resources

Overhead projector and/or flipchart and pens. Any prepared materials or handouts.

Environment

A room large enough to allow the group to work in sub-groups. An area for break time.

Timetable

1	Introduction	15 mins
2	Defining violence at work	15 mins
3	Employer duties and the need for action	1 hour
	BREAK	15 mins
4	Taking steps to safety	1 hour
5	Action planning	30 mins
6	Summary/evaluation	15 mins

Contents

1   Introduction

- Introduce yourself and the training programme, using the aims and objectives.
- Ask group members to introduce themselves.
- Give any housekeeping information, such as break time, finishing time, location of facilities, and so on.

2   Defining violence at work – a brief input session

- Explain that the term 'violence' is used in a broad sense, encompassing a wide range of behaviour and the effects of it.
- Using prepared overhead projector slides or a flipchart, show them definitions used by others – or develop your own to show them (see Chapter 4).
- Identify for the group why having a definition of violence at work is useful and important.

3   Employer duties and the need for action

- Ask the group what they believe to be the legal duties of an employer to ensure safety.
- Using prepared handouts, overhead projector slides or a flipchart, show the group a list of their duties under the Health and Safety at Work Act and Common Law, and the risks of civil actions against them (see Chapter 5 and Handout 3). Compare with their list – how accurate are they?
- Ask the group what they believe the consequences of not taking action to ensure employee safety are:

    - in legal terms;
    - in terms of the effects on the organization.

Record responses on the flipchart or overhead projector slide – offer ideas or add things they miss.

BREAK – 15 mins

4   Taking steps to safety

- Explain that the Health and Safety Executive booklet *Preventing Violence to Staff* proposes a seven-step action plan for combating violence at work, and what the steps are – write them up on the flipchart or overhead projector slide beforehand (see Chapter 5 and Handout 5).
- Go through each step with the group, explaining what it involves and why it is important. Ask for the group's views on how (or whether) they could take each of the steps. Do they feel it is a useful approach? Can they add suggestions or ideas for their own organization(s)?

5   Action planning

- The action plans should describe actions that will be taken, by whom, or who will be responsible for seeing they are taken, and the timescales.
- The actions could range from a management meeting to discuss combating violence at work to hiring a consultant to investigate risks and make proposals.

- The action plans should be achievable, and people encouraged to follow up with each other to check on progress.

6   Summary/evaluation

- Summary: go back over the key learning points from the programme:
  - a broad definition of violence at work;
  - the need for employers to act to combat violence at work because of their legal obligations, and the effects of violence at work on the organization and individuals;
  - action planning;
  - the seven-step approach to an action plan on violence at work;
  - action decided upon by participants.

- Evaluation: conduct a brief evaluation using a form or group activity, focusing on key areas such as:
  - most significant learning points;
  - what else they would like to know or do;
  - effectiveness of materials, trainer, and so on.

- Explain what further evaluation will be undertaken, and how.

Task 3 Coping with violence

Aim

To equip staff with basic skills in coping with violent behaviour towards them.

Objectives

At the end of the programme participants will be able to:

- identify a range of violent behaviour;
- describe potential triggers to violent behaviour;
- describe the signs of impending violent behaviour;
- identify a range of actions they could take in the event of being faced with a violent person;
- explain the control trilogy as a process for coping with non-physical violent behaviour (see Chapter 16).

Time

One day initially, with follow-up practice sessions.

Target groups

'Front-line' staff who deal regularly with the public, customers or clients.

Resources

Overhead projector and/or flipchart and pens, prepared handouts and other materials, such as briefs for role-players and observers.

Environment

A room large enough to allow the group to work in sub-groups, or provide additional rooms for this.

Timetable

1	Introduction	30 mins
2	What is violent behaviour?	1 hour
BREAK		15 mins
3	Causes and signs of danger	45 mins
4	What to do when faced with violence	1 hour
BREAK FOR LUNCH		1 hour
5	The control trilogy	$2^{1}/_{4}$ hours
6	Action plans	30 mins
7	Summary/evaluation	30 mins

Contents

1   Introduction

- Introduce yourself and the training programme, using the aim and objectives to explain the content and outcomes.
- Ask the group members to introduce themselves.
- Explain 'housekeeping' arrangements, such as meal times, breaks, where facilities are, and so on.

2   What is violent behaviour?

- Using a simple exercise, such as a brainstorm, get the group to identify behaviour that is violent. Record these on the flipchart.

- Explain that the term 'violence' is being used to describe a wide range of behaviour (rather than using other words, such as aggression, abusive behaviour, rudeness, harassment) of both the physical and non-physical type (see Handout 2).
- Ask the group if they can now add to the original list of violent behaviour – help them if necessary.
- Using the working definitions of violence (see Chapter 4 and Handouts 1 and 4), if you wish, ensure that the group has a shared understanding of behaviour that constitutes violence, and its effects.

BREAK – 15 mins

3   Causes and signs of danger

- Causes of violence – lead a group discussion, having posed the question 'Why do people become violent?' The discussion should identify a range of possible causes, from drunkenness and drug-taking to frustration or anger because of poor service.
- Identify the most likely causes of violence in the workplace(s) of group members.
- Signs of danger – explain to the group that it is both verbal and non-verbal communication that signals impending violence (see Chapter 15). Verbal threats or suggestions of violence are readily recognized. However, verbal signals are generally much rarer than non-verbal, so recognizing non-verbal signs of danger is important.
- Get the group to identify non-verbal signs of danger; this is often most effectively done by asking volunteers to demonstrate anger or frustration by giving them a short role-play exercise.
- Review the role-play (or other activity you may use), and either write up a list of the behaviour identified as danger signs or provide the group with a prepared handout based on the text.

4   What to do when faced with violence

- Distinguish between physical and non-physical violence and explain that after lunch they will learn one method that can help in coping with non-physical violence.
- Physical violence – explain that the options when facing physical attack are:
  - getting away;
  - fighting back – fighting free;
  - defusing the situation.

Ask the group how they would get away, fight back or try to defuse the situation. For each, use the text (see Chapter 16, pp.129–33) to explain good safe practice and to explain why some of the ideas they may have are actually likely to put them at greater risk.

- Develop with the group (or use a prepared handout) a list of key points to remember in the event of physical attack.
- Someone is likely to raise the issue of self-defence; ensure they are clear of the pros and cons of learning and attempting to use self-defence.

BREAK FOR LUNCH – 1 hour

5 The control trilogy

- Introduce the control trilogy as a useful method for helping deal with non-physical violence; make sure the group remember they do not have to try to cope if it is safer not to do so, and that they are clear that the control trilogy should not be assumed to always be appropriate or. successful.
- Using the text (and handouts you prepare from it), go through each of the stages – calming, reaching and controlling – explaining its purpose, what it involves, answering questions, discussing points, and so on.
- Give the group time to read the material you have provided, and clarify the points.
- Set up a practice exercise using role-play outlines you have prepared that are relevant in the group's working environment, and allow them to practise the stages of the control trilogy.

Trio exercises work well for this kind of practice, with three roles: the violent person, the subject, and an observer. Each of the group members (A, B and C) gets the chance to play each role. Table T3.1 shows how it works.

Table T3.1 Control trilogy – trio exercise

	Violent person	Subject	Observer
Time period 1	A	B	C
Time period 2	C	A	B
Time period 3	B	C	A

You need to make clear that there are three time periods, and they need to be about 20 minutes each. You need to brief the observers on what to look for (changes in behaviour, what worked or did not, and so on).

- Review the exercise, picking out key learning points, what the group felt about the method, what worked and did not work, how the group feel they could or would use the method.

BREAK – 15 mins

6   Action plans

- Ask the group to individually prepare an action plan identifying what they will do to implement what they have learnt, for example:
  - What will they do differently?
  - How will they use what they have learnt to help them recognize danger and cope with possibly violent people?
  - What will they avoid doing?

- With the whole group – or those who wish to do so – work out a timetable for further practice of the control trilogy.

7   Summary/evaluation

- Summarize the key learning points from the day either verbally or written up on an overhead projector, flipchart or handout.
- Using an evaluation exercise questionnaire, ask the group to identify, for example, what has been:
  - most useful/least useful;
  - well done/not so well done;
  - most enjoyable/least enjoyable;
  - most relevant/least relevant;

  and what they will:
  - use at work/not use;
  - use in their personal life/not use;

  and what they would have liked:
  - more of/less of;
  - to include/to exclude.

- Explain any further evaluation process that you wish to conduct with them.

Task 4 Communication skills

Aim

To enable learners to develop communication skills that will help them avoid or cope with violent situations.

Objectives

At the end of the programme participants will be able to:

- describe how self-awareness and the awareness of others contributes to effective communication;
- explain what is meant by 'body language' (see Chapter 15) and its importance in communication;
- explain what is meant by assertiveness (see Chapter 17 and Handout 7);
- demonstrate assertive communication.

Time

One day.

Target groups

All staff, but particularly those who regularly deal with the public, clients, customers and other colleagues.

Resources

Overhead projector and/or flipchart and pens; any prepared materials and handouts (for example, comparisons of types of behaviour, list of 'rights'; see Chapter 17, pp.135–9).

Environment

A room large enough for the whole group to split into smaller groups for practice or, preferably, separate rooms or further space for practice sessions.

Timetable

1	Introduction	30 mins
2	Non-verbal communication	$1\frac{1}{2}$ hours
BREAK		15 mins
3	Assertiveness – introduction	$1\frac{1}{4}$ hours
BREAK FOR LUNCH		1 hour
4	Assertiveness – practice	$3\frac{1}{4}$ hours
5	Action plan	15 mins
6	Summary/evaluation	30 mins

Contents

1   Introduction

- Introduce yourself.
- Use a brief exercise to enable the participants to introduce themselves.
- Introduce the programme, using the aims and objectives to describe the content and outcomes.
- Explain any 'housekeeping' arrangements, such as break times, finish time, where facilities are located, and so on.
- Make clear to the group there are benefits of effective communication in dealing with difficult or potentially dangerous situations, and risks in not paying attention to what and how we communicate.

2   Non-verbal communication

- Explain the importance of non-verbal communication, or 'body language', in communication as a whole, and why it is important to understand it in order to avoid or cope with difficult or violent situations.
- Discuss with the group the possible effects of impressions and stereotypes we all have. Ask them for examples from their own experience to show both the risks and possible advantages of these.
- For each of the elements of body language identified in Chapter 15 (dress, listening) select a method of conveying to the group its importance and effects in non-verbal communication. For example, in relation to dress, you could show them pictures and ask them about the wearer of the clothes; for facial expression or body posture, you could ask volunteers to demonstrate (as in charades) feelings to the group; for voice, you could ask several people to say the same thing in different ways; for listening, you could demonstrate the difference between active listening and just being there.
- Sum up the session by asking the whole group to complete a list of:

  - positive non-verbal communication they could adopt;
  - non-verbal 'danger' signals they will look out for.

BREAK – 15 mins

3   Assertiveness – introduction

- Explain that assertive behaviour is a learned 'positive' behaviour, and that it involves recognizing and respecting the rights, feelings, needs and opinions of self and others. It is not about getting your own way all the time.
- For each of the behaviour types described in Chapter 17 and Handout 7 (aggressive, passive, manipulative and assertive) identify with the group:

  - what each behaviour is characterized by;
  - the effects of the behaviour on others.

  You could ask the whole group to identify characteristics and effects initially, and then add to it. You could create four sub-groups and ask each of them to take one of the behaviours, identify the characteristics and effects, and feed their results back to the whole group, where everyone could add to their work; or each sub-group could consider all four behaviour types and then compare results.

- Summarize the key points that distinguish assertive behaviour as an effective and positive form of communication.

BREAK FOR LUNCH – 1 hour

4   Assertiveness – practice

- Explain the rights of individuals and the importance of remembering that we and others have the same rights; also why remembering our rights and those of others is important (see Chapter 17, pp.138–9).
- For each of the areas of communication (from making requests to feedback; see Chapter 17, pp. 139–47), or those most relevant to the group, explain how to communicate assertively in each area, or ask them for their ideas of assertive approaches and add to them through discussion in the group.
- In order to practise assertive communication you could provide role-play outlines for the group to work through, or you could ask them for examples of real-life situations from the work setting that they could practise on.
- Once the group has had the opportunity to practise, review with them what they have found difficult or easy, and identify what are the key points of assertive communication that must be remembered.

5   Action plan

Ask each group member to prepare an action plan for themselves, outlining what action they will take to implement their learning about:

- non-verbal communication;
- assertive communication.

They may then explain their plan to another group member or a sub-group, who could help clarify or expand their plan.

With the whole group (or those who wish) agree a timetable for further practice of assertive communication.

6   Summary/evaluation

- Summarize the main learning points from the day – either verbally or as a prepared written list – or ask the group to contribute to a list you compile together, if time permits.
- Conduct an evaluation, using a form or group exercise that will provide information about what the group perceived as:

  - of greatest value;
  - most useful to them at work;

- should be kept/should be dropped;
- most/least interesting or enjoyable;
- well done/not so well done;
- most/least difficult.

● Explain any further or follow-up evaluation you plan to conduct.

Task 5 Developing a policy and procedures

Aim

To encourage and enable managers (and others involved) to develop policies and procedures to protect employees from violence.

Objectives

At the end of the programme the participants will be able to:

- develop a draft definition of violence relevant in their workplace;
- identify the duties of employers in respect of safety from violence at work;
- identify areas of potential risk within their own organization;
- describe the elements of a policy on violence at work;
- draft a policy for the organization;
- develop procedures necessary to implement the policy.

Time

Two days.

Target groups

Policy-makers, managers or others involved in the development of the policy on violence, for example personnel staff, health and safety staff, management and employee representatives on health and safety committees.

Resources

Flipcharts, pens and/or overhead projector. Handouts and other prepared materials.

Environment

A room large enough to allow the whole group to work comfortably, and space or separate rooms for sub-groups. Where managers and policy-makers are involved, it is as well to be away from the workplace to avoid interruptions.

Timetable

Day 1

1	Introduction	1 hour
2	Defining violence at work	1 hour
BREAK		30 mins
3	Duties of employers	$1\frac{1}{2}$ hours
BREAK FOR LUNCH		1 hour
4	Identifying risks at work	2 hours
BREAK		15 mins
5	Summary/looking forward	45 mins

Day 2

1	Introduction	15 mins
2	Policy development	$3\frac{1}{2}$ hours (includes 30 mins break taken as appropriate)
2	Policy development (continued)	
BREAK FOR LUNCH		1 hour
3	Developing procedures	$1\frac{1}{2}$ hours
BREAK		15 mins
4	Action plans	45 mins

5   Summary/evaluation   45 mins

Contents

Day 1

1   Introduction

- Introduce yourself.
- Ask the participants to introduce themselves – they will almost certainly know each others' names and roles as they are from the same organization, so design an activity to get them to know each other better and start working together.
- Explain any 'housekeeping' arrangements, such as start and finish times, break times, location of facilities, and so on.
- Using the aims and objectives, explain the purpose, content and outcomes of the programme, stressing the practical outcomes for their organization.
- Select key research findings and other information from the text (see Chapters 1–3 and Handout 9) to demonstrate that there is a growing body of evidence that confirms that violence at work is a problem as well as that the problem is on the increase.

2   Defining violence at work

- Explain to the group what a working definition of violence is, its purpose and why it is important (see Chapter 4 and Handout 1).
- Develop a group definition (draft organizational definition), either by:

  - setting sub-groups the task of coming up with definitions, and then discussing these in the whole group to come to a group definition. You can then compare with the example in the text and refine if necessary;

  or:

  - showing the group the example working definitions, discussing these and working as a whole group towards a definition that meets their needs and those of their organization.

BREAK – 15 mins

3   Duties of employers

- Pose the group (or sub-groups) the following questions (see Chapter 5 and Handout 3):

  - What are the duties of employers in relation to the safety of staff from violence?
  - What are the costs of not fulfilling the duties (see Handout 4)?

  Either record the responses of the whole group or get each sub-group to record their answers. If you work with sub-groups, ask them to feed back their answers to the whole group.

- Using prepared overhead projector slides, a flipchart or handout from the text, compare the groups' answers to the information in the text (see Chapter 5):

  - How accurate were they?
  - Did they realize the extent of the duties upon them as employers?
  - Were they aware of the action that could be taken against them as employers/individuals?
  - Did they identify the possible costs to individuals and the organization of not tackling problems of violence to staff?

  Ask the group to identify where they feel they do and do not fulfil their duties.

BREAK FOR LUNCH – 1 hour

4   Identifying risks at work

- Remind the group of what they said before lunch about how far they believe they do or do not fulfil their duties as employers:

  - Can they be sure, if there has been no systematic or thorough investigation?
  - Would employees generally share their view?

- Explain the types of activity that have associated risks, using the Health and Safety Executive's categories (see Chapter 6):

  - How many of the organization's activities fit into the categories?
  - What other activities does the organization undertake that may have associated risks?

- Where to investigate?

  - Explain the idea of an audit as a means of investigating risks (see

Chapter 6).

- Select a number of areas worth investigating relevant to the particular organization, and ask the group members to identify questions or concerns about these areas they would want to investigate.

Discuss the questions and concerns they identify, adding to or amending their lists from the text (see Chapter 6) as appropriate, or from the ideas of the rest of the group.

- How to investigate? Discuss with the group the questions posed in the text:

  - What information do you want?
  - What form of information do you want?
  - How much information should you collect?
  - Who should conduct the investigation (see Handout 11)?

It is important that they are able to consider these questions before getting into the detail of individual methods.

- For each of the methods of collecting information described in the text (see Chapter 6):

  - describe it briefly if necessary;
  - ask for views of the advantages and disadvantages of using the method, adding information as required;
  - ask the group to say which methods they believe would work best for them and why;
  - ask if they have any other ideas of methods that may work well in the organization or part of it.

BREAK – 15 mins

5 Summary/looking forward

- Summarize the key learning points from today's sessions either for the group or with them.
- Outline the timetable for tomorrow, explaining how the work from today links to the work on developing policy and procedure.

Day 2

1 Introduction

Introduce the programme for the day, explaining that the purpose of the morning's activities is to produce a draft policy for the organization and the afternoon will focus on developing outline procedures necessary to support the policy. In both these activities they will be drawing on learning from Day 1.

2   Policy development

As this is a long session, it is advisable to take a 30-minute break when you feel the group needs it.

- Ensure that the group is clear what is meant by a policy, and what its purposes are.
- Using the headings from the text (see Chapter 7 and Handout 12), identify the areas normally covered by a policy and, briefly what each of these covers. These areas may or may not suit the particular organization's requirements, so may need to be changed – one or more left out and/or others added. Agree with the group the areas their draft policy will cover.
- The whole group could attempt to draft the whole policy, but this may prove very difficult. A more effective approach could be to set up three or four sub-groups, each of which takes responsibility for producing a first draft of a number of the policy areas.
- Once the sub-groups have completed drafts of their areas of the policy, they return to the whole group. In the whole group each policy area, starting at the beginning, can then be taken in turn and discussed, amended, added to or otherwise developed until a final draft is agreed.
- Sub-groups can then write up the final draft of the policy areas they are responsible for.
- Discuss and agree with the group the process for taking the draft policy forward in the organization, for example:
  - Who will take responsibility for typing, copying, circulating the draft, and so on?
  - Who needs to see the draft?
  - What sort of consultation process is necessary?
  - What will be the timescale?
  - Who will be responsible for overseeing policy development from here on?

BREAK FOR LUNCH – 1 hour

3   Developing procedures

- The group yesterday identified possible risks at work, and have now drafted a policy. The next step is to consider the procedures required to implement the policy and tackle the potential risks of violence they have identified.

They will probably need more information (from an investigation of some sort) in order to be precise about procedures; here they are developing proposals for the procedures they believe are likely to be required.

- Using the examples of the sorts of procedure likely to be required, ask the group to identify where they believe the organization needs:

  - to develop new procedures;
  - to change existing procedures;
  - to abandon current procedures.

  Record their responses.

- Once you have a list of their responses, help the group to prioritize the needs by identifying, for example:

  - areas of greatest risk that require urgent attention;
  - actions that can be taken immediately to deal with obvious risks;
  - cost-effective action to which there will be no resistance;
  - changes that may meet with resistance for some reason and will require consultation with, or the persuading of, others;
  - areas where no action can be taken without further investigation.

- Discuss and agree with the group how their proposals can or will be used:

  - Who will be responsible for writing them up/presenting them?
  - To whom should they go?
  - Should they accompany the draft policy?
  - Should they be kept to a later stage of the policy development process?

BREAK – 15 mins

4 Action plans

- Individuals draw up their own action plan, identifying:

  - action they have agreed to take on behalf of the group to further its work on this programme;
  - action they will take immediately in their role to minimize the risk of violence to themselves and others;
  - action they will take individually to further support the development of policy and procedures;
  - action they will take to further develop their own knowledge and skills in relation to combating violence at work;
  - timescales for their actions;
  - help or support they require.

- In pairs, trios or small groups, each person takes it in turn to explain their action plan; others can help them, for example by adding to the plan, clarifying points, offering support, or agreeing to review their progress with them at a later stage.

5 Summary/evaluation

- Summarize the key learning points from the various sessions in the programme with the group (or for them), verbally or as written notes.
- Using a form or group exercise, evaluate the programme, including aspects such as:

  - Content: appropriateness; relevance; depth; variety.
  - Style: participation/listening; active/inactive.
  - Time: length of programme; duration of sessions; length and timing of breaks.
  - Materials: quantity; quality; range.
  - Trainers: approach; confidence with subject; presentation.
  - Venue: facilities; comfort; access; refreshments.

Task 6 Practical steps to safety

This programme is designed for particular groups of staff with particular needs because of the risks they face – for example, reception staff, travelling staff, staff who work in others' homes or premises, staff who handle money or dispense drugs, and so on. The first part of the programme is common, while the second part of the programme differs, depending upon the group being trained.

Aim

To provide participants with practical knowledge of steps they can take to keep safe.

Objectives

At the end of the programme the participants will be able to:

- identify potential areas of risks in their work;
- describe practical steps they can take to keep safe in the course of their work;
- develop an action plan describing the steps they will take:
    - to change the way they work;
    - to bring about changes in procedures to ensure safety;
    - to obtain help, support and resources they need.

Time

One day.

Resources

Overhead projector, flipchart and pens, prepared materials and handouts.

Environment

A room large enough to allow space for sub-groups to work, or separate rooms.

Timetable

1	Introduction	30 mins
2	Violence at work and its effects	30 mins
3	The risks of violence	1 hour
BREAK		15 mins
4	Practical session 1	$1^1/_2$ hours
BREAK FOR LUNCH		1 hour
5	Practical session 2	2 hours
BREAK		15 mins
6	Action plan	30 mins
7	Summary/evaluation	30 mins

Contents

1   Introduction

- Introduce yourself.
- Ask participants to introduce themselves, using a name game or similar warm-up exercise.
- Explain the content and outcomes of the programme, using the aims and objectives.

2   Violence at work and its effects

- Ask the group what behaviour they would describe as violence at work, including any examples from their experience.
- Show the group the working definitions of violence at work from the text (see Chapter 4 and Handout 1) and discuss them, for example:
  - whether or not they agree with them;
  - if they are wider definitions than they expected;
  - if they cover the areas of behaviour and effects the group think they should.

- Agree a working definition with the group so that everyone is clear about the basis from which the group is working.

3   The risks of violence

- Using the research material in the text (see Chapters 2–3 and Handout 9), select examples to illustrate the increasing recognition of violence at work as a problem. Discuss with the group whether they agree with the research findings or not, and why they think violence may be on the increase.
- Explain, using figures from the text (see Chapter 2), the risks of crime. Ask the group if the statistics are what they expected, or very different. Ask if they feel they are at risk from crime and, if so, why.

BREAK – 15 mins

4 and 5   Practical sessions 1 and 2

These sessions should be designed to meet the needs of the particular group and use the material appropriate to the areas of activity and tasks that the group identifies. (Break for lunch between sessions.)

- Work with the group through the activities and tasks they perform, and the way they perform them, to identify the risks they face in relation to each.
- Ask the group for ideas or suggestions as to how they could do their jobs more safely and what support, equipment, resources, and so on they need in order to do so. Add to their ideas using materials.
- Depending upon the number of areas of activity or tasks the group identifies, set up sub-groups and ask each group to develop good practice guidelines for one or more of the activities or tasks identified.
- Feed back the good practice guidelines to the whole group, adding to

them or amending them as the group members contribute their ideas and observations.

BREAK – 15 mins

6 Action plan

- Each individual should identify in their action plans:
  - tasks or activities they will perform differently to minimize any risks to them;
  - support, help, equipment and so on they will try to obtain in order to make their jobs safer;
  - how they will try to bring about any changes in procedure/practice to minimize the risk of violence at work;
  - further information, advice or training they feel they need, and how they plan to go about obtaining what they need.

Ask the group members to try to build in timescales, and to find others in the group to support them in achieving their action plan and/or help them assess their progress at an agreed point.

7 Summary/evaluation

- Summarize the key learning points from each of the sessions during the day for the group, or ask the group or sub-groups to develop a summary of the sessions for discussion and add to it in the whole group.
- Evaluate the programme to obtain immediate reactions, such as:
  - how relevant the group felt it was;
  - whether it was practical enough;
  - what more would they have liked;
  - what they would keep the same or change.

- Explain to the group when and how any future evaluation of the programme will take place.

Appendix A

Sample handouts

These handouts can be prepared in advance of training sessions, for distribution to participants. They can also be used to prepare transparencies for use with overhead projectors.

Handout 1: Definitions of Violence

- 'Any incident in which an employee is abused, threatened or assaulted by a member of the public in circumstances arising out of the course of his or her employment.' (Health and Safety Executive's working definition of violence, 1988.)
- 'The application of force, severe threat or serious abuse by members of the public towards people arising out of the course of their work whether or not they are on duty. This includes severe verbal abuse or threat where this is judged likely to turn into actual violence; serious or persistent harassment (including racial or sexual harassment); threat with a weapon; major or minor injuries; fatalities.' (Department of Health and Social Security Advisory Committee on Violence to Staff, 1988).
- 'Behaviour which produces damaging or hurtful effects, physically or emotionally, on people.' (Association of Directors of Social Services, 1987).

Handout 2: Examples of Violence

Physical violence

- assault causing death
- assault causing serious physical injury
- minor injuries
- kicking
- biting
- punching
- use of weapons
- use of missiles
- spitting
- scratching
- sexual assault
- deliberate self-harm.

Non-physical violence

- verbal abuse
- racial or sexual abuse
- threats – with or without weapons
- physical posturing
- threatening gestures
- abusive phone calls
- threatening use of dogs
- harassment in all forms
- swearing
- shouting
- name-calling
- bullying
- insults
- innuendo
- deliberate silence.

Handout 3: Employer's duties (Health and Safety at Work Act, 1974)

The general obligation: 'it shall be the duty of every employer to ensure so far as is reasonably practicable, the health, safety and welfare of all his employees'. The matters to which that duty extends includes:

- 'The provision and maintenance of plant and systems of work that are, so far as is reasonably practicable, safe and without risk to health.'
- 'The provision of such information, instruction, training and supervision as is necessary to ensure, so far as is reasonably practicable, the health and safety at work of his employees.'
- 'The provision and maintenance of a working environment for his employees that is, so far as is reasonably practicable, safe and without risk to health.'

In addition there is an obligation to draw up and publish written safety policies to include these matters. Apart from the obligations under the Health and Safety at Work Act, there are other obligations on an employer arising from:

- The employer's duty of care under Common Law for the safety of his employees.
- The employer's duty under any nationally negotiated agreements.
- The employer's duty not to dismiss employees unfairly. Employees have resigned in some situations and successfully alleged constructive unfair dismissal because the employer failed to provide reasonable precautions for the employee's safety, thus establishing a precedent.

Handout 4: Effects of violence on staff

Any form of violence, whether or not it results in some sort of physical injury, can have serious effects on the workforce, including:

- high levels of anxiety;
- stress-related illness;
- absenteeism and the need to cover for staff;
- low morale;
- high levels of staff turnover;
- low productivity;
- little job satisfaction;
- low employee involvement;
- industrial action or poor industrial relations;
- difficulty in recruiting and retaining staff.

Handout 5: Developing an action plan

- Step 1: Find out if there is a problem.
- Step 2: Record all incidents.
- Step 3: Classify all incidents.
- Step 4: Search for preventive measures.
- Step 5: Decide what to do.
- Step 6: Put measures into practice.
- Step 7: Check that measures work.

Handout 6: Signs of danger

In dealing with others, watch for the following:

- raised voice, rapid speech and gabbling, as this signals rising tension;
- changes in tone and pitch as the conversation progresses that may suggest anger, frustration or impending violent behaviour;
- slow, menacing tones that, despite the words themselves, demonstrate that the speaker is angry and likely to erupt into violent behaviour.

Handout 7: Some characteristics of aggressive, manipulative and passive behaviour

AGGRESSIVE	MANIPULATIVE	PASSIVE
Recognizing own rights only	Avoiding direct approach	Acting as a 'doormat'
Forceful expressions of opinion	Covert expressions of views	Failure to express views
Need to prove superiority	Skills at deceiving	Decision-making problems
Giving orders rather than requests	Need to be in control	Blaming others
Blaming others	Not trusting self or others	Resignation
Putting people down	Denial of feelings	Giving in
Not listening to others	Insincerity	Saying 'yes' – meaning 'no'
Competitiveness	Making veiled threats	Complaining behind the scenes
Verbal abuse, insults	Using guilt as a weapon	Not knowing own boundaries
Over-reacting	Sabotage behind the scenes	
Egocentricity	Using derogatory language	
Threats	Talking behind people's backs	

Handout 8: Characteristics of assertive behaviour

Assertive behaviour is characterized by:

- self-respect and self-esteem;
- respect for others;
- recognition of your own and others' rights;
- acceptance of your own positive and negative qualities and those of others;
- acknowledging your own responsibility for your choices and actions;
- recognizing your own needs, wants and feelings, being able to express them, and allowing others to do the same;
- listening to others;
- being able to ask for your own needs to be met and risk refusal;
- accepting that you do not always get what you want; feeling rejection but not being destroyed by it;
- open and honest interaction with others;
- knowing your own limits; ability to say 'no' and respect others' limits or boundaries;
- giving feedback or constructive criticism when it is due, accepting it of yourself if valid, or rejecting it if it is not.

Handout 9: Some research findings

- In 1987 the Health and Safety Executive's Health Service Advisory Committee produced a report which suggested that violence to health service staff was far more common than previously believed. In some areas of work violence to staff was a regular occurrence. A survey of 3 000 health service workers showed that in the previous year:

  - 0.5 per cent had an injury requiring medical assistance;
  - 11 per cent had a minor injury requiring first aid;
  - 5 per cent had been threatened with a weapon;
  - 18 per cent had been threatened verbally.

- The TUC's report on *Violence to Staff* in 1988 highlighted the lack of a comprehensive body of data on violence at work. It then reviewed current initiatives on violence to staff in a range of employment sectors, and showed that awareness of the problem had increased but the nature and extent of the risks to employees was still unclear.

- The 1988 report of the Department of Health and Social Security Advisory Committee on *Violence to Staff* concluded that the issue should be considered in the wider context of service provision and against the legal background of the Health and Safety at Work Act 1974. The report made recommendations for all DHSS services and argued that central strategies alone are insufficient; initiatives must take into account local circumstances. Where strategies for combating violence have not been developed the report proposed urgent action, even in certain services or areas where violence is not perceived as a problem.

- In 1988 the *British Crime Survey* (BCS) found that teachers, welfare workers and nurses are three times more likely than the average employee to be verbally abused or threatened. Other occupational groups with a similarly increased risk of abuse include managers in the entertainment sector, transport workers, male security guards and librarians.

- Phillips, Stockdale and Joeman, found that:

  - 8 per cent of people are likely to suffer an assault on their journey to

or from work;
- 20 per cent are likely to experience an unpleasant incident on their journey;
- 20 per cent face threatening behaviour;
- sexual harassment occurs most frequently, with 20 per cent of victims being women in professional occupations where they spend a substantial amount of time away from a base, or workers in shops and offices;
- the frequency of physical attacks ranges from a relatively low 4 per cent for female office workers to approximately 15 per cent for male professionals who often work away from the office;
- the incidence of experiencing threatening behaviour varies from 10 per cent among office-based professionals to 33 per cent for those who often meet clients.

- The *British Crime Survey* for 1988 showed that 25 per cent of crime victims said that the incident had happened at, or because of, work. Fourteen per cent of respondents said they had been verbally abused at work at least once in the previous year, and approximately 33 per cent of all threats of violence were received at work;
- Research published in 1987 by the Labour Research Department was largely concerned with public services and showed that:

    - 98 per cent of workplaces had experiences instances of abuse or harassment;
    - 85 per cent of workplaces reported that threats of violence had been made;
    - 62 per cent of workplaces suffered one or more instances of actual violence, including 80 per cent of transport companies and 77 per cent of health authorities;
    - 28 per cent of workplaces had experienced violence using a weapon.

- In the survey of 210 workplaces with a total of over 86 000 employees, 67 per cent felt that the level of abuse and violence had increased during the past five years.
- The IDS Study 458 (May 1990) found that transport and hospital staff in particular are especially at risk late at night and at weekends. Hospital casualty departments find that the vast majority of assaults are clustered late on Friday and Saturday nights, when they are busiest.
- The *Which? Report on Street Crime* used the British Crime Survey as its basis because of the belief that it was a better indicator of crime rates than police statistics. The BCS figures show that:

- the likelihood of being mugged, even in a high-risk area, is less than the 20 per cent chance of having a car or some of its contents stolen in a year;
- mugging is more common in inner-city, multi-racial areas, council estates with low-income tenants and areas with 'non-family' housing (that it, from bed-sits to large detached properties);
- men are more at risk from crime overall than women, and particularly from violent crime in the streets;
- elderly people are less at risk from crime than young people, and not simply because they go out less. It is young men who are most at risk of assault and robbery;
- Afro-Caribbean and Asian people are more likely to be the victims of crime than white people;
- Asian people are more likely to suffer vandalism, personal theft and victimization by groups of strangers.

- A West Midlands Survey in 1994 found that:

  - 63 per cent of GPs had suffered abuse;
  - 27 per cent had changed their work practice;
  - 12 per cent had struck off one or more patients because of fear of violence;
  - 11 per cent discussed aggression at practice meetings;
  - 9 per cent had installed panic buttons;
  - 7 per cent used deputizing services because of fear.

Handout 10: Where workers are at risk

The Health and Safety Executive breaks high risk jobs into the following categories:

- Giving a service: benefits office, housing department;
- Caring: nurses, social workers, community care staff;
- Education: teachers, non-teaching staff;
- Money transactions: post offices, banks, shops, building societies, bus drivers/conductors;
- Delivery/collection: milk delivery, postal services, rent collection;
- Controlling: reception staff, security staff, traffic wardens;
- Inspecting: building inspectors, planning officers.

Handout 11: Methods for information collection

Methods of collecting information include the use of questionnaires, observation, structured interviews, working groups and the use of external consultants.

Other methods which have proved effective include:

- suggestion boxes;
- use of team meetings with supervisors or managers;
- staff meetings or departmental meetings;
- asking people to write in with views, ideas, problems, opinions, and so on;
- open forums with safety or personnel staff;
- visits to other workplaces to observe different practices.

Handout 12: Areas covered by a policy on violence at work

- Policy title.
- The purpose (or aim or objective).
- Definition.
- The philosophy.
- Whom the policy covers.
- What the employer is committed to do.
- What is required of individuals.
- Performance measures.
- Evaluation/review.

Appendix B

Violent incident report form

CONFIDENTIAL

Violent Incident Report Form

To be used to report incidents which involve actual or threatened violence to staff.

Part I Report by Employee

1 *Employee:*

Name..
Job title...
Place of employment ....
Ethnicity (use agency's usual categories) ....

---

2 *Details of Incident:*

When did the incident occur?
Date........................Day ....Time On/Off Duty ....
Where did the incident occur? (draw a sketch if necessary)

What actually happened leading up to and during the incident? (attach a separate sheet if necessary)

Names, job titles, addresses of any witnesses:

---

3   *Assailant:*

Name (*if known*)..
Address (*if known*)..
....
Age...
Ethnicity ....
Other relevant information:

4   *Type of Attack:*

Verbal threat	Severe verbal abuse
Threatening posture	Written threat
Threat with weapon	Physical assault
Other (specify):	

5   *Nature and Extent of Injuries:*

Physical:

Emotional:

Treatment received, if any:

Damage to personal property, if any:

6   *Immediate Action:*

    Incident reported to:
    Police   yes/no
    Line manager   yes/no
    When was incident reported?

    Who reported the incident?

    Action taken:

7   *Employee's Comments on:*

    What caused the incident?

    How could a recurrence be made less likely?

    Other comments:

Signed   .... Job Title   .... Date   ....

Part II   Line Manager's Report

I have read the report by...and have taken the
following action:

The following further action is in my opinion needed:

Details of sick leave, if any:

Other comments:

Signed   .... Designation   .... Date   ....
(Line Manager)

Copies of Parts I and II should be sent by the line manager to the personnel
department. (N.B. An extract may be needed for the client's file.)

Select bibliography

Books and booklets

Argyle, Michael (1988), *Bodily Communication*, London: Routledge.

Arroba, T. and James, K. (1987), *Pressure at Work: A Survival Guide*, London: McGraw-Hill.

Ashworth, Henry (1981), *Assertiveness at Work*, New York: McGraw-Hill.

Birmingham City Council Women's Unit (1989), *Facing Aggression at Work*, Birmingham City Council.

Braithwaite, R. (1992), *Violence, Understanding and its Prevention*, Oxford: Radcliffe Professional Press.

Breakwell, G. M. (1989), *Facing Physical Violence*, London: British Psychological Society and Routledge.

Collins, David J., Tank, Manju and Basith, Abdul (1993), *Customs of Minority Ethnic Religions*, Aldershot: Arena.

Davies, Jessica (1990), *Protect Yourself*, London: Judy Piatkus.

Department of Health (1993), *Guidance on Permissible Forms of Control in Children's Residential Care*, Heywood: HMSO.

Dickson, Anne (1986), *A Woman in Your Own Right: Assertiveness and You*, London: Quartet Books.

Egan, G. (1990), *The Skilled Helper*, London: Brooks/Cole.

General Medical Services Committee (1994), *Combating Violence in General Practice*, London: BMA.

Hanmer, J. and Saunders, S. (1984), *Well-founded Fear – A Community Study of Violence to Women*, London: Hutchinson.

Health and Safety Executive (1975), *Health and Safety at Work etc. Act, The Act Outlined*, London: Free from HSE.

Health and Safety Executive (1988), *Preventing Violence to Staff*, London: HMSO.

225

Health and Safety Executive (1990), *A Guide to The Health and Safety at Work etc. Act 1974* (4th edn), London: HMSO.

Lamplugh, Diana (1988), *Beating Aggression – A Practical Guide for Working Women*, London: Weidenfeld and Nicolson.

Lamplugh, Diana (1991), *Without Fear – The Key to Staying Safe*, Abertillery: Old Bakehouse Publications.

Leicestershire Family Health Services Authority in conjunction with Leicestershire Constabulary, *Protecting General Practice*, Leicester: Leicestershire FHSA.

Library Association (1987), *Violence in Libraries*, London: Library Association.

National Association of Health Authorities and Trusts (1992) *NHS Security Manual*, Birmingham: NAHAT.

Phillips, C.M. and Stockdale, J.E. (1991), *Violence at Work – Issues, Policies and Procedures*, Luton: Local Government Management Board.

Schneider, V. and Maguire, J. (1993) *Violence at Work and its Impact on the Medical Profession Within Hospitals and the Community*, London: BMA.

Suzy Lamplugh Trust (1994), *Violence and Aggression at Work: Guidance for Employers on Principles, Policy and Practice*, London: Suzy Lamplugh Trust.

Suzy Lamplugh Trust (1994), *Personal Safety at Work: Guidance for All Employees*, London, Suzy Lamplugh Trust.

Suzy Lamplugh Trust (1994), *Fast Guide to Personal Safety at Work*, London: Hascombe Enterprises.

Woods, M. and Whitehead, J. (1993), *Working Alone – Surviving and Thriving*, London: Pitman.

Articles

Adcock, J. (1988), 'Prevention of violence to staff', *Local Government Employment*, October.

Braithwaite, R. (1988), 'Coming to terms with the effects of violence', *Social Work Today*, 20 October.

Braithwaite, R. (1992), 'Running away is OK', *Social Work Today*, 23 April.

Brockington, R. (1989), 'Violence to staff', *Local Government Employment*, August.

Caldwell, M. F. (1992), 'Incidence of PTSD amongst staff victims of patient violence', *Hospital and Community Psychiatry*, Vol. 43, pp. 838–9.

Cardwell, S. (1984), 'Aggression management: violence in accident and emergency departments', *Nursing Times*, 4 April, pp. 32–4.

Castillo, D. N. and Jenkins, E. L. (1994), 'Industries and occupations at high risk from work-related homicide', *Journal of Medicine*, Vol. 36, No. 2.

Copelend, L. (1987), 'Travelling abroad safely: some tips to give employees', *Personnel*, February.

Fottrell, E. (1980), 'A study of violent behaviour among patients in psychiatric hospitals', *British Journal of Psychiatry*, Vol. 36, pp. 216–21.

Francis, W. (1986), 'What the organisations say', *Community Care*, December.

George, M. (1993), 'Insults and injury', *Community Care*, 13 May.

Green E. (1989), 'Management of violent behaviour', *Journal of Emergency Nursing*, Vol. 15, No. 6, pp 523–8.

Hall, L. (1989), 'Attacking aggression', *Personnel Today*, May.

Harrington, J. M. (1990), 'The Health Care of Health Workers: The Ernestine Henry Lecture 1990', *Journal of the Royal College of Physicians of London*, Vol. 24, No. 3, pp. 189–95.

Hill, C. (1989), 'Protecting employees from attack', *Personnel Management*, February.

Hobbs, F. D. R. (1991), 'Violence in general practice – a survey of General Practioners' views', *British Medical Journal*, Vol. 302, pp. 329–32.

HSIB (1988), 'Preventing violence to staff', *Health and Safety Information Bulletin*, No. 154, October.

Industrial Society Information Service (1989), 'Employers liable for violence to staff', *Industrial Society Magazine*, March.

Kelly, B. (1989), 'A case of wolves in sheep's clothing', *Local Government Chronicle*, April.

King, J. (1989), 'How do you handle violence?', *Community Care*, 23 March.

Loss Prevention Council (1995), Technical Briefing Note.

Morgan, M. M. and Steedman, D. J. (1985), 'Violence and the accident and emergency department', *Health Bulletin*, Vol. 43, No. 6, pp. 278–82.

Painter, K. (1987), 'It's part of the job', *Employee Relations*, Vol. 9, No. 5.

Passmore, J. (1989), 'Violent clients – service or safety?', *Housing Planning Review*, Vol. 44, No. 2, April/May.

Roberts, M. and Hopkins, J. (1986), 'Confronting violence', *Health Service Journal*, June.

Tonkin, B. (1986), 'Quantifying risk factors', *Community Care*, November.

Whitehead, M. (1988), 'A violent war on the front line', *Local Government Employment*, February.

Whittington, R. and Wykes, T. (1989), 'Invisible injury', *Nursing Times*, Vol. 85, pp. 30–32.

Williams, B. (1988), 'Violence and risk at work', *Probation Journal*, Vol. 34, No. 4, December.

Williams, B. and Howe, A. (1988), 'Violence to staff – another possible answer', *Local Government Employment*, February.

Wills, J. (1987), 'Realising the risks', *Local Government Chronicle*, November.

Wykes, T. (1991), 'The Prevention and Management of Violence', *Institute of Psychiatry*, London.

Reports and papers

Health and Safety Executive, Health Service Advisory Committee (1987), *Violence to Staff in the Health Services*, London: HMSO.

Home Office Standing Committee for Violence (1984), *Report of the Working Group – Fear of Crime in England and Wales*, London: Home Office Public Relations Branch.

Home Office (1989), *Safer Cities – Progress Report 1989–1990*, London: Home Office Safer Cities Unit.

Phillips, C. M., Stockdale, J. E. and Joeman, L. M. (1989), *The Risks in Going to Work*, London School of Economics and Political Science Report, London: Suzy Lamplugh Trust.

Training resources

Brook Street (1987), *Smart Moves*, St Albans: Brook Street.

Cardy, C. and Lamplugh, D. (1992), *Training for Personal Safety in the Workplace*, Aldershot: Connaught Training.

Channel 4 Television (1988), *Assert Yourself*, Guild Training.

Counsel and Care (1993), *The Right to Take Risks – Model policies, guidance to staff and training material on restraint and risk-taking in residential homes and nursing homes for older people*, London: Counsel and Care.

Lamplugh, D. (1994), *Personal Safety at Work*, Cinegrade Productions.

Leeds Animation Workshop (1983), *Give us a Smile*, Leeds Animation Workshop.

Local Government Management Board (1987), *Dealing Effectively with Aggressive and Violent Customers*, Luton: Local Government Management Board.

Local Government Management Board (1987), *On the Front Line*, Luton: Local Government Management Board.

London Ambulance Service (1988), *Ambulance Services Basic Training Manual*, London.

McGraw-Hill (1982), *Communicating Non-defensively – Don't Take it Personally*, McGraw-Hill Films.

Reynolds, N. (1981), *Personal Safety*, Rank Aldis.

Social Services Inspectorate (1989), *Violence to Staff*, CFL Vision.

Suzy Lamplugh Trust (1989), *Avoiding Danger*, Creative Vision.

Suzy Lamplugh Trust (1989), *You Can Cope – Lifeskills Training Pack*, Gower Publications.

Suzy Lamplugh Trust (1994), *Violence and Aggression at Work: Resource Pack*, Suzy Lamplugh Trust.

Useful organizations

Birmingham City Council Women's Unit
Congreve House
Congreve Passage
Birmingham
B3 3DA

Tel: 0121 235 2715

British Association for Counselling
1 Regent Place
Rugby
CV21 2PJ

Tel: 01788 578328

British Medical Association
BMA House
Tavistock Square
London
WC1H 9JP

Tel: 0171 387 4499

Commission for Racial Equality
Elliot House
Allington Street
London
SW1E 5EH

Tel: 0171 828 7022

Criminal Injuries Compensation Scheme
Whittington House
19–30 Alfred Place
London
WC1E 7LG

Tel: 0171 355 6800

Equal Opportunities Commission
Overseas House
Quay Street
Manchester
M3 3HN

Tel: London – 0171 287 3953; Head Office, Manchester – 0161 833 9244

Health and Safety Executive
Baynards House
1 Chepstow Place
Westbourne Grove
London
W2 4TF

Tel: 0171 221 9178

Home Office
50 Queen Anne's Gate
London
SW1H 9AT

Safer Cities Unit – Room 583a; Public Relations Branch – Room 133

Industrial Society
48 Bryanston Square
London
W1A 1BQ

Tel: 0171 262 2401

London Rape Crisis Centre
PO Box 69
London
WC1X

Tel: 24-hour helpline – 0171 837 1600; Information – 0171 278 3959